THE MANIFEST WEALTH SAFELY METHOD

A 3-Step Guide to **Creating Wealth** While Pursuing **Purpose-Driven Passion Projects** You Love That Change The World

IKE IKOKWU

THE MANIFEST WEALTH SAFELY METHOD

A 3 Step Guide To To Creating Wealth While Pursuing Purpose Driven Passion Projects You Love That Change The World

Design and cover art by Grace Perral.

ISBN (Paperback): 978-0-9853723-1-6

To the team who supports the work I do with the MWSM in serving our clients. To my wife and kids who give me the space needed to live life in rhythm. With all of my heart and soul, thank you!

"What I love most about reading: It gives you the ability
to reach higher ground and keep climbing"

~ Oprah Winfrey ~

TABLE OF CONTENTS

INTRODUCTION

HOW TO READ THIS BOOK

This book exists for three reasons:

Reason #1:
So that you'll eventually hire me and my team to help you implement everything you read in this book.

Reason #2:
To help you Break Invisible Boundaries over what you think is financially possible to experience an abundance of wealth, not only of the financial kind, but in the 7 realms of wealth.

Reason #3:
To build credibility with you as someone who isn't teaching theory but rather sharing wisdom from results I've achieved in the past, that I'm currently achieving, and that I'm helping my clients achieve.

As you'll soon find out from the pages of this book, I'm going to be vulnerable in sharing my past wins, losses, and everything in between. I'll also be fully transparent, honest and quite frankly sometimes blunt with you through the various parts of my book.

I've heard it said that, "if you want people to believe you can help them, help them."

Simply put, I want to help you.

To accomplish that goal, I've structured this book as follows:

First, I want you to experience an epiphany on the direct correlation between being wealthy and identifying, clarifying and magnifying your purpose. It's my firm belief that you can't create, protect and perpetuate real wealth without it being tied to your purpose. You'll be completing some exercises to start the journey of identifying your purpose. I firmly believe that everything you hope and dream for in life and in business sits on the other side of your purpose.

In partnership with the WHY Institute, my WHY.os Certification empowers the work I do with my clients in helping them discover their WHY so that they can identify, clarify and magnify their purpose to live a truly fulfilled life. This in turns allows them to make purpose-driven and legacy-impacting changes in their lives so they can really impact the world around them.

Resources will be provided to you should you want to take a deeper dive beyond what's offered in this book to have a WHY.os coaching call with me to discover your WHY, HOW and WHAT. This will allow you to truly unleash your purpose and live an extraordinary life.

Second, I'll make a case for how you can shrink a traditional 30-year financial independence timeline down to as little as 5 years. And don't worry, this isn't based on theory but rather what I did when I went from bankrupt in 2003, to becoming financially independent, with a million dollar plus net worth, and six figures in passive income back in 2008 at the age of 34, which was my second time of building a seven-figure net worth.

For those who have at least $100,000 in liquid net worth, you'll discover a simple 3-step guide to use in duplicating what I did from 2003 to 2008. And, for those who have less than $100,000 in liquid net worth, you'll also discover a simple 3-step guide you can use to achieve the same results. Even if the pathways are slightly different for each group, I can assure you that the end results will be the same, especially when you learn how to accelerate the creation of wealth.

You'll learn that while there may be things you could have done better in managing your wealth, a lot of the challenges you face in achieving your financial goals are partly systemic. They are also partly based on decisions you've made following the well-intentioned advice of those you'd presume to have your best interest at heart. These include your mom and dad, as well as members of the financial services industry who go by the names financial advisors, investment advisor, insurance agent etc.

Third, I'll spend time enlightening you on why most people fail to achieve their financial and wealth accumulation goals. I'll share the top 5 reasons I've seen why this happens time and time again. Then I'll go over the 5 ways we guarantee our clients wealth success by helping them avoid the top 5 reasons for failure. And, I'll wrap up this section with: What The Manifest Wealth Safely Method can actually do for you.

Finally, I'll conclude by discussing How To Start Your Wealth Building Adventure. I'll share What You Should Do Next, How You Can Get More Help, and tell you a bit more About The Author and why you should listen to me and follow my guidance.

If you're remotely interested in discovering how to manifest wealth safely and earn 1% to 25% monthly returns so you can shrink your financial independence timeline down from 30 to 5 years while pursuing purpose-driven passion projects you love that change the world, then you've selected the right book to guide you through making that a reality in your life.

I know a lot of what I just said in the last paragraph sounds like a rather tall order. I get it, most thought it was impossible to run a 4 minute mile until Roger Bannister did so on May 6, 1954. But if you hang with me, I assure you that I'll make you a believer that not only is what I mentioned possible, it's also very probable.

The truth is, as complex a subject as this might sound, the entirety of this book can be summed up in the following three steps for each group of those who have $100,000 in liquid net worth and for those who don't.

Those three steps for those who don't have $100,000 in liquid net worth are:

Step #1:
Find a High-Income Earning Opportunity: Simply put, the quickest way to 10X your income is as an entrepreneur. This book will highlight one of the best opportunities to become an entrepreneur and build a Seven-Figure business in 2 years or less even if you know nothing about sales, marketing or technology.

Step #2:
Find a High-Growth Wealth Building Opportunity: Once you understand why Albert Einstein labelled compound interest the eight wonder of the world, you'll want to have a love affair with it, to increase the velocity of wealth creation.

Step #3:
Find a Passive Income Creation Opportunity: If compound interest is the eight wonder of the world, I believe passive income is the 9th wonder of the world. Once you understand this, you'll appreciate why Warren Buffet says "if you don't find a way to make money while you sleep, you will work until you die."

Those three steps for those who already have $100,000 in liquid net worth are:

Step #1:
Discover Your Purpose: I believe that it's more tragic to have wealth and not know why, than to have death and not know life. If you already have $100,000 in liquid net worth, you've at least taken the first step to creating wealth. What you now

want to do is accelerate the creation of wealth, but not before you discover what you'll do with that wealth. If we were all created on purpose and for purpose, then it's our responsibility to figure out what that is because as I've said before, all that we desire in life and in business, as well as the mark and impact we are to have on earth, all of that sits on the other side of our purpose.

Step #2:
Find a High-Growth Wealth Building Opportunity: Once you understand why Albert Einstein labelled compound interest the eight wonder of the world, you'll want to have a love affair with it, to increase the velocity of wealth creation.

Step #3:
Find a Passive Income Creation Opportunity: If compound interest is the eight wonder of the world, I believe passive income is the 9th wonder of the world. Once you understand this, you'll appreciate why Warren Buffet says "if you don't find a way to make money while you sleep, you will work until you die."

These 3 step guides and the entirety of the contents of this book radically changed my life for the better. The principles and concepts you'll learn are what allowed me to go from broke, busted, and disgusted in 2003, to being financially independent by 2008.

Some of the lessons learned to facilitate that comeback, I shared in my Amazon Best Selling Book, Winning The Money Game: Separating the Myths From The Truth - Everything You Don't Know About Achieving Financial Independence. That book is an excellent companion to this one. So, I'd recommend you get it at everyone's favorite e-commerce store, Amazon, or simply grab it here: **https://bit.ly/winningwithike**

When a series of business betrayals, being victimized by a ponzi scheme in 2014 in which clients of mine and I fell suffered losses at the hands of a fraudster, and an ensuing SEC complaint, in an attempt to hold me responsible for me and my clients losses, wiped out all of my wealth in 2014, it's these same principles that are helping me stage a massive financial comeback as I find myself on the path to becoming a Billionaire by the year 2026.

Above all, it is my sincere hope that you shatter every invisible boundary you've placed over what's possible for you to experience, as it pertains to the seven realms of wealth.

This book will focus on just one of those realms, financial wealth. But, true wealth does not occur unless you are also harnessing wealth within your spiritual, soulful, physical, relational, influential and social realms as well. That's what an abundant life looks like, and it's your divine right to enjoy life and to enjoy it more abundantly.

I'll be the first to admit that yes, this is a marketing book. But it's much more than a marketing book. It's a book that's going to inspire you, motivate you, challenge you, energize you and hopefully activate you to live the life you've always hoped and dreamed of.

A life where you experience an abundance of love, joy, peace, patience, kindness, goodness, gentleness, faithfulness, self-control and wealth in all seven realms of your life.

When I unpack my purpose and my WHY in later chapters, you'll understand why I'm so fired up about the legacy and impact I'm going to have while still alive on earth and even more so after I'm gone.

You'll understand why I want you just as fired up about your purpose and WHY as I am. You'll know why I'm on a mission to remove any financial hindrances from allowing you to pursue your purpose-driven and legacy-impacting changes you want to champion to make our world a better place.

Part of mine is to raise an army of 10,000 Righteous Billionaire Leaders by the year 2030 that in one word, will be world-changers with the impact they have in the seven mountains of our culture, as they restore righteous leadership at the foundations of all nations.

You'll learn more about my big WHY and purpose in later chapters and I hope it lights a fire in you as it does to me. I can't stress how important it is to discover yours for when you do, you'll find an abundance of resources to help you bring it to pass. One of those resources could be this book.

So, it's with great pleasure, privilege and honor that I get to share with you what I know, not just from the multiple licenses I've held in the past, which include a Certified Public Accountant, a Certified Financial Planner, an Investment Advisor, an Insurance Professional, a Certified John Maxwell Speaker, Teacher and Trainer, a Certified Neuro Linguistic Professional, and a Certified New Money Story Mentor Coach, but to name a few. And, not just from the Masters Degree in Personal Financial Planning or the Bachelor's Degree in Accounting.

All of those accomplishments are all well and good. The greatest distinction in my ability to help you is that I've transcended the world of theory from my degrees, certifications and licenses, entered the bloody battle of real life and done what I'm sharing here with you not once in my lifetime, but twice.

This third time, my end result will not just be a Millionaire with Six-Figures in Passive Income, but it will be a Billionaire with Nine-Figures in Passive Income who has a definite, larger than life purpose for what he'll be doing with all that accumulated wealth.

It would be an honor if you 'd join me in this all too exciting adventure. Consider this book your invitation to do so.

As a special gift to purchasers of my book and to help you accelerate your wealth success, and internalize a lot of the concepts and principles I share with you, access the additional resources I'm offering for FREE by going to **http://bookbonus.manifestwealthsafely.com**

If you read this book and decide you'd like my help implementing the strategies discussed here to help you create at least one million in new wealth and six figures in passive income in five years or less, while pursuing purpose-driven passion projects you love that change the world, then please book a call to chat with me or a member of my team by going here:

http://call.manifestwealthsafely.com

Helping people like you not only retire early but also be refired about your purpose to change the world is exactly what we do day-in and day-out.

We're here to help.

To your success,

Ike Ikokwu

"The Safe Wealth Creator"
Founder of the Righteous Billionaire Movement
Founder of the Manifest Wealth Safely Program
Founder of the Seven Figure Mentor Program

PART 1

Why **Purpose Is KEY** To Being Wealthy

CHAPTER 1

Why Early Retirement Should Not Be Your Purpose

"Retirement isn't the end of the road, but just a turn in the road"

~ Author Unknown~

Let me be one of the first to bust your bubble by telling you that early retirement is fool's gold. This should not be your purpose in life. I'll be fair and tell you that even I use early retirement as a marketing ploy because it's catchy and it gets people's attention. Heck, the name of one of my Master Classes is: How To Live Your Life on FIRE.

I like the acronym FIRE. The first time it caught my attention, it was used to convey the idea of being Financially Independent and Retired Early, which I like. As a matter of fact, I liked it so much that after becoming financially independent and retiring early in 2008, just 5 years after a bankruptcy filing in 2003, I took on the moniker, 'The Financial Independence Coach," as my clients were amazed at how I arrived 31 years early to a destination many hope to get to at 65.

Truth be told, I failed miserably at early retirement for a host of reasons. For starters, while I live on a golf course, I have no interest in engaging in a sport where I'm not getting sweaty or bumping into people as I might do playing tennis or basketball. There are many reasons why I failed at early retirement, but chief among them was that I lacked a true sense of purpose....or you could say I had a misguided purpose.

After having accomplished most of my financial goals at the tender age of 34 in 2008, without a clear sense of purpose, I simply looked for things to fill that void, and chased after more opportunities to make even more money.

Oh, I pity the fool who wishes for something he wants, gets that thing, and then, does not have the foggiest idea of what to do with it. That's a story for another time and another book of mine.

But, what came from the ashes of my failure at retiring early was a profound appreciation for the need to be clear on your purpose, and to ditch that word "retire early," and instead replace it with something more meaningful and inspiring.

Now, back to the whole idea of living your life on "FIRE." As I said before, "FIRE" is an acronym for Financially Independent and Retired Early. Now, doesn't the idea of living life on FIRE just draw you in from a marketing perspective?

Sure it does. Heck I'd be all over that Master Class myself if it came across my radar. Like I said, it's good marketing. And, I think part of the reason why the communication of that idea works so well can be found in a 2019 Gallup poll. The results of that global poll by Gallup uncovered that out of the world's one billion full-time workers, only 15% of people are engaged at work. That means an astronomical 85% of people are not happy with their work.

With that as a backdrop, you can better understand why the idea of early retirement is appealing to many. However, just because I teach on becoming financially independent and retired early, just because the idea is appealing, and just because our culture has a lot to say about early retirement, doesn't mean that you should, no matter how enticing spending the rest of your life here in this picturesque location may seem.

For starters, I don't believe anyone on planet earth was created to retire early. I mean there's a lot of intentionality within just the DNA structure of everyone that's on planet earth, that quite frankly prohibits and precludes each and everyone of you from retiring early.

There's a deposit you are to make in the lives of people. There's this thing that only you have been uniquely gifted and qualified to do and your mission in life is identify, clarify and magnify that purpose.

And when you do, your life will be filled with so much vigor, energy and passion that retiring in the traditional sense is something you'd never even contemplate.

I mean...Why would you retire from something you love doing, something that inspires you, that taps into the wildest part of your creativity, that gives life to you and that is life giving to others?

Just doesn't make any sense, right? And therein lies the problem...most people haven't found their purpose, or they haven't allowed their purpose to find them.

So rather than retiring early on the beach, wouldn't you much rather live your life on FIRE?

F - Financially
I - Independent
R - ReFired
E - Early

I mean REFIRED about your purpose…

I mean REFIRED about that thing you've been uniquely gifted to do…

That thing which will allow you to make the greatest contribution you are supposed to make on this side of heaven.

As you're reading this, just nod your head up and down if this speaks to you, if you'd like to live your Life on FIRE.

Wonderful...In my mind's eye, I can see you nodding your head up and down. So, thank you for that.

Do me a favor. If you could do absolutely anything in the world that you know would give you the greatest amount of fulfillment...what would that be? Would you:

- » Inspire others?
- » Maybe go on local and international speaking tours?
- » Write and become an author?
- » Maybe unleash your creative side that perhaps is laying dormant in what you're presently doing?
- » Spend more time supporting charitable causes and becoming part of something special?
- » Start a business?
- » Launch a non-profit of your own?

Go ahead, grab your journal and make a note of how you'd choose to make a difference in the world doing something that would be really fulfilling to you.

It's important to make note of this.

You know, if you felt something in your heart, a sweet sensation, as you were thinking about an answer to this question, chances are that's something you can and should get RE-FIRED about.

And, if you're not already doing this thing, one of the many reasons why, quite honestly, might be the lack of an abundant flow of money into your life. Am I right or am I right?

If you're nodding your head up and down again, you're in luck. By the time you're done with this book, I'm going to show you how to change that, so money flows freely and abundantly into your life. And when that's happening, I'm willing to bet you'd be able to unlock the door to truly doing that which fulfills you in the depths of your soul.

I want to encourage you with a little dose of my reality so you can get a sneak peek into what's possible for you. Right now, I'm loving the heck out of life as I pursue my purpose as expressed in the work that I'm doing at www.righteousbillionairemovement.com This is work that I'm deeply committed to, that I'm passionate about and that is extremely fulfilling to me.

I make a decent amount of money as a Business Strategist, Financial Coach and Mentor to my clients. But, if I never worked another day in my life, it would not significantly impact my well being. How so, I hear you wonder? It's because I've implemented a lot of what you'll be discovering in this book so that my money works harder for me than I work for it.

It's the fourth quarter of 2021 as I write this book and at present, if I did nothing to generate active income, I'd still enjoy a high four-figure a month in passive income that would translate to six figures in passive income for the year. I have my money allocated in pre-ipo stocks that over the next 3 to 12 months will provide 200% to 500% returns on the capital we have allocated. In 2022, my monthly passive income will be five figures a month and in 2023 it will balloon to six figures a month.

And, the best part is I don't have to lift a finger to accomplish any of that passive growth in my wealth and my income. When you learn to leverage the secrets of top financial institutions and the UBER wealthy, when your circle of influence opens doors to opportunities normally reserved for people with nine-figure net worths, you can gain access to opportunities to passively earn as little as 1% to as much as 25% per month on the capital you have deployed to certain wealth accumulation opportunities. And when you do that, you significantly increase the velocity of wealth creation.

But don't just take my word for it, here are a few words from clients of mine that are a part of the Righteous Billionaire Movement and that are participants of my Manifest Wealth Safely program.

Just how successful has our **Manifest Wealth Safely Program** been in helping clients earn as little as 1% to as much as 25% per month on their money so they can shrink their financial independence timelines down from 30 years to as little as 2 to 5 years?

Very Successful!

Dave Sheets

Entrepreneur, President of Outlaw Sales Group, Colorado Springs, Colorado

"I was a financial advisor with Merrill Lynch for, you know, a year and a half. And so, I got, to know, fairly deep into a lot of the instruments that are out there. And I've never seen anything like this. And, you know, five percent doesn't compare to twenty five percent. But, when you take five percent over a year and multiply that out, I mean, you're looking at 60 percent growth, which is incredible"

Gabe Hoover

Teacher, Coach, Entrepreneur, Founder & CEO of YouByDesign, Dublin, Ohio

"But over the last 10 days in the program you set me up in Ike, I've made 6% in 10 days. And after getting the account all set up and everything, to be hands off and not have to be a daily trader and just know that the system is working for me, that was, that was both eye opening and encouraging"

Judy Whalen

Entrepreneur, Founder, & The CEO of Whalen & Associates, and The Center for Strategic Change, Brooklyn, Wisconsin

"So now I'm in this program, I have to tell you, it's a hoot! It's actually, it's fun! So, in less than 14 days, I'm up 5.6%. I haven't earned 5% at a bank in years."

Kevin Hailstock

Entrepreneur, Founder and CEO of Web Emerse, LLC, Washington DC

"So, totaling up, a little over five percent for my close to 12 days in the system."

Lois Koffi

Top 20 Podcast Host, Professional Speaker, Sales Trainer & Coach, Entrepreneur, Founder, & The CEO of Lois Koffi Enterprises, Vista, California

"Perhaps you'd share a little bit about some of the 'inside scoop' as to what you've seen so far? Oh my gosh, well last month it was 16 plus percent. This month it's been 6.5% percent and growing. You know, I'm all about data and hard numbers and you've been very transparent about showing how this is possible. And yes, there's no guarantees, I get all that. But you have a track record, you have other clients who have a track record"

Dave, Kevin, Judy, Gabe and Lois all have an idea of the kind of impact they want to have in the world. And, as they will gladly share with you, the picture of what's possible for them to be, do and have is getting clearer by the day, as they embrace the idea that they can have their money working harder for them, than they've been accustomed to working for it.

They are all on their individual paths of identifying, clarifying and magnifying their purpose. And while each of them could take early retirement in just a few years, I assure you that from what I know about them, that's not even something they are contemplating as they are getting REFIRED about their purpose.

In the next chapter, we'll get into who this book and the message contained in this book is really for. But first, here are a few chapter reflection questions for you.

FOR REFLECTION:

1. Do you get more excited for the weekend when Friday rolls around or do you get more excited about the work week when Monday rolls around?
2. Do you absolutely love the work you do today?
3. If money was not an issue and you could do absolutely anything in the world that would bring you total fulfillment, what would you do?
4. Are you more excited about being retired early or being refired early?
5. What kind of impact would it have on your life and that of those you love if in the next two to five years you were financially set for life?

CHAPTER 2

Who This Book (and Message) Is For?

"Coming together is a beginning, Keeping together is progress; Working together is success. Life is not accumulation, it is about contribution. You're happiest while you're making the greatest contribution."

~ Tony Robbins ~

The method you are about to discover in this book was born from some of the darkest moments of my life. Moments that at the time were deeply painful, but today, I have a profound appreciation for how those moments shaped who I am today. I've mentioned before that I've made and lost a seven-figure net worth twice. I want to give you a peek into both of those moments.

My First Seven Figures

After graduating college in 1996 with my degree in Accounting, I worked for two of the Big 6 accounting firms at the time, KPMG and Ernst and Young and within their Personal Financial Solutions Group, I got exposed to some pretty cool strategies that were being used to perpetuate wealth, while minimizing tax burdens of the high net worth families of the closely-held businesses we served.

It was immensely enlightening work I was doing at these firms. As someone who's been curious about money since the days when I was 8 years old and using my dad's old briefcase as a make-shift bank for all the money I was "stacking" at

Christmas when our extended family rewarded the children for good scholastic achievement in school that year, I was like a kid at the candy store.

While I didn't have as many zeros in my bank account as the clients I served, after all, I was only making like $50,000 at the time, I've always had a knack for learning new things and implementing the knowledge gained. The early years in my career would be no different.

In my spare time outside of work, I started investing in real estate and making $30,000 to $50,000 or more per deal. Not too long after that, I had stacked multiple six figures in capital, while sitting on about a dozen rental properties in the Atlanta area.

My appetite for wealth and curiosity about money, led to being exposed to offshore investments. At one point in my 20's, I had "control" of an International Business Corporation in Panama, an offshore trust in Belize, and banking accounts in Latvia. With this exposure, I got into Bank Debenture Trading Programs and High-Yield Investment Programs that were touted as being shrouded in secrecy, as they generated high double digit returns on a monthly basis.

Young, naive, easily influenced, and motivated by greed, I parlayed a lot of the profits I'd made from real estate investing into these offshore investments. The returns were phenomenal and while I was only making $50,000 on my job, I was making 5 times that much from my investments. One of my friends who I got into real estate investing with, introduced me to the guy providing access to these high-yield investments. And when he explained what they were to me, honestly, I didn't understand them, but since my friend was "all in and making money," I figured, what the heck, I'd jump in as well.

WIth exponential growth in my net worth and income, it didn't take long for me to ditch our fully functional and fully paid for vehicles, for "His and Hers Mercedes S-430 and SLK 230," that set us back about $150,000. And, oh that townhouse that I had almost paid off, we'd ditch that and go into $500,000 in debt on a 2.3 acre 5,000 square foot home to house not a family of 5, but just a family of 2, since it was just my wife and I at the time. Money and greed will make you do some really dumb stuff!

Did I mention that the returns from these investments were great? Well, they were, while they lasted. That is, until they were uncovered as a massive scam and the Canadian mastermind behind it was prosecuted and sent to jail for engaging in what's adequately described as a scam at this site here: **https://www.quatloos.com/stkscams/hyips.htm**

This offshore investment started to unravel right around 9/11. Not only was the United States reeling from the terrorist attacks, but the stock market was crumbling at death defying speed. It was at around this same time that I lost my employment at one of the largest financial brokerage firms in Atlanta, because a fellow employee was "jealous" of the wheeling and dealing I was doing on my lunch breaks with my real estate investments.

So, here I am, with my offshore investments cratering, my domestic investments plummeting thanks to the Tech Bubble, my income disappearing, due to being severed from work, and oh, the tenants in my rental properties, they all of a sudden couldn't pay their rents anymore. I was hit with the trifecta of financial blunders, and after not being able to find employment for 18 months, my wife and I would file bankruptcy and start over.

There were lots of lessons learned from this special time in my life. I'll share three of them now:

» **LESSON #1:** Stewardship: Never let a sudden abundance of cash flow impair the sound financial stewardship decisions you've made in life.
» **LESSON #2:** Greed: Be aware of the subtle but insidious impact that greed can have on you.
» **LESSON #3:** Knowledge: Never invest in something you don't understand, at least at a fundamental level. Warren Buffet has been a stickler on that rule for a while and with good reason. We'd take heed

to "Know Thy Investment."

After licking the wounds from this "special time" in my life, God revealed to me that the reason why someone who had an impeccable resume would go through 18 months of unemployment, and couldn't even pay an employer to hire him, was because my purpose and destiny was not as an employee, but rather was as an entrepreneur. Unlike many "born entrepreneurs" out there, I was actually forced into entrepreneurship by the Big Guy upstairs.

My Second Seven Figures

God apparently had good reason why my destiny was as an entrepreneur and not an employee, as over the next 5 years from 2003 to 2008, not only would I more than 10X my $50,000 a year salary I made as an employee, but I'd step into 2008 with over a seven figure net worth and $100,000 in passive income, much of which was tax-free. The details of how I accomplished that feat led to the release of my Amazon best selling book: Winning The Money Game, which I mentioned in the Introduction you could pick up at Amazon.

After I released my book in 2012, it appeared to the outside world that I was at the top of my game. Young and financially independent, with a Best Selling book, tons of media coverage from your favorite TV, radio, and print media sources, and a growing and thriving investment advisory and financial services practice. What more could a guy want or ask for, right?

Well, that's just the problem. I wanted more success and more wealth so I kept looking for businesses to buy and other things to keep me busy because "winning" and "achieving" had become like a drug to me and while I seemed like I was winning to the outside world, I was dying a slow death on the inside.

I'm not sure what your spiritual frame of reference is but mine is rooted in my relationship with the Trinity as a Christian. My heavenly father took notice of the deterioration that was occuring on the inside of me and while he didn't orchestrate the next "special moment" in my life, I know he allowed that moment to happen to mature me in my faith for the next epic chapter of my life.

In 2014, my whole world unravelled. I suffered two significant business betrayals in which my family lost over seven figures of wealth and we saw our income drop to about a third of what it used to be. To make matters worse, one of the business betrayals was a classic Bernie Madoff type ponzi scheme, except our fraudster fled the country and was never brought to justice.

While reeling from the losses I suffered in 2014, I'd get the pleasant news 2.5 years after this incident, that the SEC had decided to file a complaint against me and my companies, in an attempt to hold me responsible for both me and my investment advisory clients losses at the hand of the fraudster who fled the country.

It's my contention that since this wasn't a $50 Billion dollar fraud, it was "only" $200 million and since there were no celebrities impacted by this fraud, the SEC decided not to expend the resources necessary to track this fraudster down and bring him to justice. Instead, they chose to neglect the $600,000 plus my family lost in the fraud and attempt to hold me responsible for me and my client's losses.

So, this kicked off a legal battle in which I asked the SEC to respectfully reconsider their opinion about their complaint against me and my companies, since like my clients, I was also victimized by the fraudster. They wouldn't budge. After six figures in legal expenses and almost 2 years of my life, I was quickly running out of money and we hadn't even gone to trial at this point in 2018.

After some gut-wrenching consultations with my legal team, we made the decision to settle my case with the SEC on a neither admit nor deny basis. As part of that settlement, I agreed to have my investment advisory license suspended with the right to reapply for it in the year 2023. My CFP license was also suspended with the right to reapply in the year 2023. I also paid out over $320,000 to settle my case with the court appointed Receiver and the SEC.

I stepped into the ring for a modern day rendition of David versus Goliath, with me playing the part of David and the SEC as Goliath. And, while I didn't have the resources that Mark Cuban had to overpower Goliath when he went to battle with them in a case of his own, I did have a promise from God that I would experience victory in my fight against the SEC.

Judging from the outcome of my case, with my financial resources depleted, my income below the poverty line, my investment advisory business dead, and my reputation ruined with the very flattering comments the SEC, and media outlets had to say about my case, I think you'd agree with me that this looked nothing like the victory I'd been promised by my Father in heaven.

And, like any good son would do, I asked my Father why he reneged on His promise to me and his response floored me. He said, "Son, you are experiencing the victory that I promised you, but the problem is you expected a 'public victory' where you got to keep your assets, income, reputation and business. However, what you needed was an internal victory."

He went on to say that, "While the loss of income, assets, and reputation were significant, the most significant loss was the loss of your identity as my son. Your identity had become so wrapped up in how much money you'd accumulated and what successes you'd achieved in life, that you forgot that your value to me is rooted in who you are as my son, and not what you do."

As I continued to dialogue with Him, he said that, "As far as victory goes my son, here's where the internal victory has taken place. In the almost 25 years of marriage to your wife Emma, you are finally loving her the way she's yearned to be loved. With your children, you're finally 'present' in their lives. As a result of my grace, you now recognize that your self-worth will alway be infinitely greater than your net worth. And, the beauty of this is you're just like a lot of my other 'kids' out there, who've lost a real sense of who they are. So, I've allowed you to go through this because on the other side of it, you'll be able to help my other kids get healing from the identity crisis they are suffering and how that's hindering them from experiencing the abundant life I've destined for them to have."

IT Had To Happen

As I've reflected on both of my experiences of making and losing over a seven-figure net worth twice in my life, I've come to the conclusion that IT HAD TO HAPPEN! What is your It? Your "it" is whatever that thing was, that setback, that thing that happened in your life, that when it happened, you looked at the rest of your life and you said, "Oh my God! Life as I know it will never be the same"

When I think back on the second time that I lost over seven figures and how my battle with the SEC had me on the precipice of filing bankruptcy again, during the first half of 2019, and I see how God's providence and favor completely turned my situation around and had my coaching and consulting business doing the monthly equivalent of six figures by the end of 2019, I know that IT had to happen!

When I look at the loss of assets, income, business, and my reputation, I realize that "IT" had to happen. That "IT" was necessary to prepare me for what I'm doing now. As I sit and reflect on the launch of the Righteous Billionaire Movement I started in 2021. It's a movement that's going to create and raise an army of 10,000 Billionaire Leaders by the year 2030.

Billionaires who are not only going to have the leadership capital through the training, coaching and mentorship we provide through the Manifest Wealth Safely Program, but leaders who will have the financial capital to literally be world changers.

Leaders who will step into every sphere and mountain of our culture, as they eradicate wickedness and evil, and as they restore righteousness back at the very foundation of our nation, to make our nation, and all nations, great again.

As I reflect on all of that, I'm fully convinced that IT had to happen. Why? Because the level of adversity that you face in life is commensurate with the level of destiny that God has planned and purposed for your life.

There's a reason why Joseph in the Bible had to go through 13 years of being falsely imprisoned, being lied about and waiting and waiting and waiting for the moment, the Kairos moment, when it was necessary, when it was time, when he was ready to step into the fold and become the second highest ranking official in the nation.

"IT" had to happen to Joseph because he had to be prepared for the magnitude of purpose and destiny that was on his life. The reason he got the dreams that he got was because there was so much that he was going to do. And, to prepare him for that, he had to go through those seasons of adversity.

That's why the Bible says to count it all joy when you're faced with trials and tests and things that absolutely don't make any sense, because you've got to pass the test of perseverance.
Are you willing to persevere, to see the dream, the goals and the hopes that you have for yourself and your life come true? "IT" had to happen; so, do me a favor today. As you think about your situation, you think about the difficulties and challenges that you're faced with, look at yourself in the mirror and say: "IT" had to happen. "IT" is for your good. "IT" is preparing you for the next level of greatness and destiny that is over your life.

There were lots of lessons learned from this special time in my life. I'll share three of them now:

- **LESSON #1:** Identity: Our identities should never be rooted in our "human doing". It should always be rooted in our "human being," and for me, my being is that of a child of God, the Creator of the Universe. A child who is immensely loved, cherished and celebrated by his Father in Heaven.
- **LESSON #2:** Adversity: We have to let adversity be our greatest mentor in life. And remember that your greatest opposition always knocks on the door of your greatest opportunity. The pathway to the greatest privileges we desire in life is spelled "pressure." How we handle pressure and adversity determines everything in life.
- **LESSON #3:** Greatness: The truth is greatness and brilliance have always been in you. It's been there even before you were formed in

your mother's womb. The question is are you willing to go through the refiner's fire for your greatness to be revealed to the world?

Who's This Book For?

Now that you know a bit of my background, now that you know a little about the seasons of adversity I've been through and some of the lessons I've learned, I want to share who this book and message is for. From the testimonials you read about in Chapter 1, you can see that I serve Founders, CEOs, Executives, Teachers, Working Professionals, Self-Employed Individuals and Entrepreneurs. Let me offer some more nuances about who I serve and who are great clients for the kind of work I do. They fall into these five categories:

1. 40 to 60 year old working professionals who as a result of what we'll call the 'storms of life,' you feel like you are behind the proverbial '8-Ball' when it comes to planning for a secure financial future.
2. 30 to 50 year old Entrepreneurs and Founders of companies who are purpose driven by nature, and want to diversify, and create wealth outside of their growing companies, wealth that can feed some of their other purpose-driven passion projects they love.
3. 40 to 60 year old Christian entrepreneurs and working professionals who sense a significant call of God on their life to advance the Kingdom, who resonate with the vision of **www.righteousbillionairemovement.com** and want to increase the velocity of wealth creation for their family, as they identify, clarify and magnify their purpose here on earth.
4. 40 to 60 year old Coaches, Consultants, Course Creators and other "Experts" who transitioned from Corporate America years ago to pursue their entrepreneurial dream, but are looking for a way to expedite the growth of wealth they built in their old 401Ks, that are now IRAs, and are looking for options on accelerating their active, passive and residual income generation.
5. Executives who were displaced as a result of the pandemic and who would love to explore a high income earning opportunity to be in business for themselves but not by themselves, while serving a highly

desirable niche of small business owners that have both the need and financial capacity to compensate you well for helping them grow their business.

In the next chapter, we'll get into the importance of knowing your WHY. But first, here are a few chapter reflection questions for you.

FOR REFLECTION:

1. What has been your greatest failure in life?
2. What do you perceive to be your "IT" that had to happen?
3. How has "IT" shaped who you are today?
4. Do you sense purpose and destiny connected to your "IT"?
5. Could a creative expression of your purpose be reflected in you becoming an entrepreneur?

CHAPTER 3

The Importance Of Knowing Your WHY

"Very few people or companies can clearly articulate WHY they do WHAT they do. By WHY I mean your purpose, cause or belief - WHY does your company exist? WHY do you get out of bed every morning? And WHY should anyone care?"

~ Simon Sinek ~

I work with Executives, CEOs, Founders, Entrepreneurs, and Working professionals who are leaders in their own right, as well as really brilliant people. And, what I've found is that those who are at the top of their game, and who keep reaching for new heights in life, are those who have absolute clarity of their WHY and are able to articulate their purpose.

Mark Twain said it best when he shared with the world this important truth: The two most important days in your life are the day you were born and the day you find out why. I believe that life doesn't really start until you discover your WHY. It's the single most important determinant of success and fulfillment in life that I've found.

A 2014 article from the Harvard Business Review noted that: "Academics argue persuasively that an executive's most important role is to be a steward of the organization's purpose. Business experts make the case that purpose is the key to exceptional performance, while psychologists describe it as the pathway to greater well-being. Doctors have even found that people with purpose in their lives are less prone to disease"

With the evidence mounting on the importance of discovering your WHY, that same article noted that "in their work of training thousands of managers at organizations from GE to the Girl Scouts, and teaching students and executives at Harvard Business School, they found that fewer than 20% of leaders have a strong sense of their own individual purpose. And, even fewer could distill their purpose into a concrete statement."

As far as I'm concerned, to live life without clarity of your WHY and an ability to articulate your purpose is like having the key to the most sophisticated computer that can solve all of life's problems and yet not knowing where that key is.

If not knowing your WHY was like a secret cancer that was killing you from the inside, would you want to do something about it? I sure hope so.

Here are 5 reasons why not knowing your WHY can be detrimental to you:

» **Anxiety:** Knowing your WHY is like having a compass to your life. If you've ever experienced the stress of going on vacation to a destination you've never been before and forgetting your map or directions (way before GPS was a thing), then you know how stressful that can be. Your life is filled with intention to get you to a specific destination. Knowing your WHY is like having the map for that trip.

» **Shiny Object Syndrome:** Less than 2 years after the September 11 attacks against the United States, our country invaded Iraq amid accusations from the Bush administration that Saddam Hussein had ties with al-Qaeda terrorists and that he had chemical and possibly biological weapons, and the potential for developing a nuclear bomb. To encapsulate how dangerous this was, it was referred to as Weapons of Mass Destruction (WMD). In the world in which we live in today, one of our greatest threats to success in squeezing out every ounce of potential in us is what I would call Weapons of

Mass Distraction aka the shiny object syndrome. When you know your WHY, you can avoid the modern day equivalent of WMD's.

- **Lack of Motivation**: If you're looking for a key driver to success in life, look no further than motivation. Think back to the things you've been most successful with in life and you'll find clear motivation for accomplishing those things. And, when you look at the things you've not been successful with in life, you'll also find a lack of motivation. Nothing keeps you motivated as having clarity on your WHY.

- **Lack of Growth**: As the great John Maxwell is quoted as saying, "Change is inevitable. Growth is Optional." In other words, by the mere passage of time, you will change. You'll transition from being a child to becoming an adult, to becoming a spouse, and then a parent, and grandparent. While those changes will naturally occur, whether or not you grow wiser through those transitions is optional. Once you know your WHY, growth is no longer optional, it's intentional.

- **Lack of Fulfillment:** You were created on purpose, by purpose, and for purpose. The only reason I can think of why the Gallup global poll of worldwide workers showed that 85% of employees were not engaged at work, code word for them not being fulfilled, is because I firmly believe they don't know their WHY. Nothing adds more meaning and fulfillment to your life than knowing your WHY. Simply put, it's your reason for being.

If knowing your WHY was like an elixir to all of the problems in life, when would you want to discover your WHY? Here are 5 benefits of knowing your WHY:

- **Simplicity:** Let's face it, life can be very complicated. It's been said that "adulting" is hard. There's an increasing array of demands being placed on us daily. One of the benefits of knowing your WHY is returning to a place of simplicity in life. Your WHY mandates the decisions you make. Once you know where you're going, you know what roads won't take you there. Purpose defines your "address." It shows you your destination, which is where we get the root word destiny. Purpose leads you to your destiny. Your destiny dictates your decisions which makes it easy to say "No" to things that are not in alignment with your destiny, which in turn helps you avoid the shiny object syndrome. That brings an immense amount of simplicity to your life.

» **Peace:** One of the biggest reasons people are stressed is from not knowing what to do. Once you've unpacked your WHY and figured out your address in life, you know your destination. You know what you're destined for. It becomes easy to make decisions that are in alignment with where you are headed. To avoid a lot of the stress and anxiety many feel, all you have to do is discover your WHY.

» **Joy:** When you're not stressed and anxious about where you're going in life or what you're supposed to do, you're instead engaged in the kind of work and activities that are in alignment with your destiny, which in turn fills your heart with joy knowing that you are doing exactly what you were created to do.

» **Growth:** John Maxwell has already taught us that while change is inevitable, growth is optional. There's nothing that motivates someone to be intentional about personal growth as a leader in their home, at their job, at their business, or in their community, as knowing your WHY. It's an innate incentive to maximize your full potential.

» **Fulfillment:** A quote you might hear from me often is this: "The examined purpose-driven life is the only life worth living." With data from the Gallup poll indicating that 85% of our workforce is unhappy and unfulfilled, the ultimate elixir to this is to do like Simon Sinek says and "Start With Why." Once you are intentional about examining your life and discovering your purpose, you'll find the one true life worth living.

To further underscore the importance of knowing your WHY, when you think about the game of golf, who's name comes to mind? For me, it's Tiger Woods. How about tennis? For me Serena Williams, Roger Federer, and Rafael Nadal come to mind. What about basketball? Michael Jordan, and Stephen Curry are the two names that come to mind. How about talk show hosts? Oprah Winfrey springs to mind for me. Online Shopping? Jeff Bezos. Electric cars? Elon Musk. Actors? Denzel Washington for me.

It really doesn't matter what your responses were to these questions. But the point is whomever was top of mind for you in response to each question were likely people who are extremely successful in their field. None of that success happens by chance. None of the great achievements were coincidental. They were strategic and intentional.

I said it before and I'll say it again here: Everything you've ever hoped and dreamed for sits on the other side of discovering your WHY and unpacking your purpose, your vision and your goals. So let me share my WHY with you so you can see an example from someone who isn't a household name like Bezos or Jordan, yet!

Through my strategic partnership with the WHY Institute, I learned that my WHY is to Make Sense of the Complex and Challenging. I love taking things that are difficult and complex and solving them, to help other people understand them so they make sense to them. That's me at my best. I'm a problem solver.

But not only did I Learn my WHY, I learned my HOW and my WHAT. My own personal WHY operating system. My HOW is to find a Better Way and share it with others. And my WHAT is to Clarify. Let me put that all together for you. Here is my personal WHY.os Statement:

I believe that success happens when we Make Sense of the complex and challenging. HOW I do that is by finding better ways and sharing them with others. And ultimately WHAT I bring are Clear solutions to help others move forward faster. And that's why what I'm doing with writing this book is very important...showing you how to shrink a 30 year financial independence timeline down to as little as 2 to 5 years as you identify, clarify and magnify your purpose.

I think you'll agree with me that shrinking a 30 year financial independence timeline down to as little as 2 to 5 years is a rather complex matter. Part of my purpose is to show you a better, more efficient way to do so, and to bring clarity on how to get there faster. I believe getting there in 2 to 5 years versus 30 years qualifies as getting there faster, don't you?

When I went through the WHY.os process and unpacked my WHY.os Statement, it completely resonated with me. I have found that every time I have been at my best, is when I am living my WHY. It's when I am making sense of the complex, finding better ways and sharing them, and delivering clear solutions. That is exactly what I am doing here today. I am taking something complex, and helping you Make Sense of it. I have found a Better Way of doing it, and I am sharing it with you. And at the end, I am providing a Clear plan for you to move forward.

And therein lies the power of knowing your WHY and even more importantly discovering your WHY.os Statement. If you want to know your WHY at a deep level and discover the profound impact that having clarity on your WHY.os Statement can have on your life, then you're really going to love what I've arranged for all of the purchasers of my book. It's an opportunity to do a deeper dive into your WHY and discover your Personal or Business WHY Operating System, at an exclusive online experience just for purchasers of my book.

When I conduct these WHY Discovery and WHY Operating System (WHY.os) Statement Coaching sessions for Executives, CEOs, Founders and other Leaders, I charge $2,500 for these 'in person' sessions. There's now an online virtual experience of the same process that retails for $500. However, since you've already made an investment in my book, I've made special arrangements for you to go through the online experience and have a call with me for just $197. That's a whopping 92% OFF the normal price others are paying for the same thing.

Simply go to this URL: **http://whyos.manifestwealthsafely.com** to get 92%

OFF to go through this online experience, plus have an hour coaching call with me to know your WHY at a deep level and discover your WHY.os Statement. By going through this online experience to discover your Personal or Business WHY Operating system, you'll get to:

1. Uncover the internal operating system that drives your decisions and direction.
2. Identify your unique gifts, where you best fit in the world and how to live with passion knowing your Personal WHY.os.
3. Reinvigorate your team/family or business by discovering each individual's operating system and talents and how those talents can best serve your business/family.
4. Create new external messaging that best attracts your ideal customer and delivers predictable results.

Discovering Your Personal WHY Operating System (WHY.os) Coaching calls retails for $2,500 daily. But again, to add value to purchasers of my book, you're getting this at 92% OFF.

I hope you take advantage of the resources provided in this chapter to discover your Personal or Business WHY.os. If there were ever such a thing as having an unfair advantage in life, I believe the insights from your WHY.os will provide such an advantage.

In the next chapter, I'll show you a 5-step process to discover your life purpose. But first, here are a few chapter reflection questions for you.

FOR REFLECTION:

1. Have you discovered your WHY?
2. Can you communicate your WHY in a clear and convincing statement?
3. Are you motivated and fulfilled by the work you do daily?
4. What can you do about the things in your life that repeatedly stress you

out and that minimize your opportunity for constant growth?

5. Have you attended the Personal or Business WHY.os experience and if YES, did the results resonate with you? And, what insights did you gain?

CHAPTER 4

A 5 Step Process To Discover Your Life Purpose

"Discovering your purpose is the most significant thing you will do in your life, and you, your loved ones, and the world will be better off because you went on this journey"

~ Mastin Kipp ~

In our last chapter, we talked about the importance of knowing your WHY. In this chapter I'm going to unveil a 5 step process to discover your life purpose. But, before I do, it's important that I also highlight the importance of knowing your life purpose. And, we'll start that discussion off with a question for you.

Here it is: What's the most intoxicating high you've ever had in life? Was it:

A. Smoking ganja?
B. Getting drunk?
C. Falling in love?

I've smoked ganja before but like former President Clinton, I didn't inhale (cough, cough). There's no doubt that one of my most intoxicating highs has been falling in love. I ate, slept and drank thoughts about my first real love.

I was consumed by her and couldn't stop thinking about her. I'd go to bed thinking about her, stay up late and have conversations with her. I'd lose sleep after being up late talking to her. I'd wake up early with thoughts about her on my mind. It was overwhelming, but in a good way. I was punch drunk in love, and thankfully, I ended up marrying her.

Those same overwhelmingly good feelings, those same moments, they are all recreated for you when you find your purpose. And, unlike a quick hit from ganja when you inhale, not that I know anything about that? But, rather than the high lasting for a few minutes, this high can last forever.

Once you experience this feeling, your whole life begins to make sense. It's like you found the owner's manual to life and you understand how the puzzle pieces fit together. There may be false starts to finding your purpose or your purpose finding you.

But, this much I know, once you find it or it finds you, it's like a turbo twin engine now powering your life. It's why I'm passionate about working with purpose-driven entrepreneurs. It's why I love helping others discover their purpose.

And speaking about purpose, here's mine: My purpose is to be a catalyst and change agent for others to unleash their infinite potential and destiny to an extraordinary life...a life by design and not by default.

A life where, if you feel you've been dealt a bad hand, you realize that you can simply shove those cards to the middle of the table, step into the role of the dealer, and deal yourself a new set of cards.

My purpose is why I'm passionate about the work we're doing with the Righteous Billionaire Movement. It's my reason for being and it's why I believe that life doesn't start until you discover your purpose or it discovers you. It's why with good reason Simon Sinek says you should Start with Why.

Our Why at the Righteous Billionaire Movement is to raise up the next generation of Billionaire Leaders. Leaders who have both the leadership and financial capital to be disruptors who make righteous changes within our nations.

Changes which restore righteousness at the foundation of the seven spheres of culture. Changes which set a lasting precedent of what purpose-driven servant leadership can look like. Changes which raise the leadership lid of those in positions of power. Changes which make nations great again!

It's a really BIG WHY and honestly, I don't know the full details of how it will all come together

But…

I sure as hell am excited to find out how it all unfolds. What does your owner's manual say? What is your driving force in life? What is your big idea? Have you discovered your purpose? Or, has it discovered you?

Here's a quote from one of my favorite authors, speakers, pastors, business coaches, mentors and thought leaders, the late Dr. Myles Munroe:

"It's more tragic to be alive and not know why, than to be dead and not know life"

That quote kind of hits you right in the eyes, doesn't it? This quote is why you've heard me say: "The examined, purpose-driven life is the only life worth living." If you and I are both in agreement with these two stellar quotes then let's do something about it.

Let's not just exist on this side of heaven, be content living an ordinary life, and be OK with the idea that 85% of the working population can be disengaged and unfulfilled with the work they do. Let's make a commitment to live an extraordinary life. Let's avoid this tragedy that the late Dr. Myles Munroe speaks of. Let's maximize each and every breath we take and truly make the life we live seem magical to the average person.

Here's the 5 step process to discover your Life Purpose. It's the 5 keys to avoid the tragedy Dr. Munroe speaks of. And, it revolves around having an awareness of the 5 critical questions you must answer while taking up space on earth.

Those 5 questions and the 5 steps are:

» **Who – Who are you?:** At the very core of your fiber, do you really know who you are? And, do you love who you are? We spend so much of our time and energy with an outward focus, trying to learn so much about things and people we forget to get really curious about who we are. This reminds me of my Car Tag in College that said: "Know Thyself." And, like an onion, God's been peeling back the many layers to help me discover who I really am.

» **Where – Where are you from?:** Your place of origin is important. It's not a determinant of your final destination in life, but it certainly has clues for you to be aware of. When I look at my place of origin and birth in Africa, the home of Kings, when I look at my Grandfather who was widely recognized as a Warren Buffet of his time, and when I look at our pedigree, it speaks volumes about my destination in life.

» **Why – Why are you here?:** Why are you taking up space on earth? The fact that you woke up with breath in your lungs means you are here by purpose, on purpose and for purpose. What is that? Use the "MAT" Acronym to unveil what motivates you, what angers you, and what transformation you want to bring and teach to the world and chances are, you'll unpack your Why and do like Simon Sinek says…Start with your Why. It's the key to every open door you need to do bigger and better things in life.

» **What – What are you capable of?:** This speaks to capacity. The Bible says the whole world waits in eager expectation for the sons and daughters of God to be revealed. What are you supposed to be revealing to this world? What would you do if you knew every real, perceived, or imaginary limitation was broken off your life? What would you do if you were really willing to bet on yourself?

» **When – When will you take action?:** Once you step into an awareness of the greatness that lies within you, the next question is when are you going to release that greatness to the world? An old ancient Chinese proverb says: The best time to have planted an apple tree was 20 years ago. The next best time is today, right now. So don't delay in releasing your greatness and your brilliance to the world.

So, answering these 5 questions can help you avoid the tragedy that Dr. Myles Munroe referred to in his quote. It honestly is the most important thing you can do in life. And when you do it, you, your loved ones, and the entire world will be better off because you were intentional in taking this journey.

Additionally, these questions represent the 5 step process to discover your life purpose.

In the next chapter, I'll show you a 5 step process to discover your business purpose, so you know what kind of business to start and run. But first, here are a few chapter reflection questions for you.

FOR REFLECTION

1. Who are you?
2. Where are you from?
3. Use the MAT acronym to answer the question: Why are you here?
4. What are you capable of?
5. When will you take action?

CHAPTER 5

A 5-Step Process To Discover Your Business Purpose

"But sometimes a particular purpose can be squared with a particular career. It may take nothing more than reexamining your career, asking some questions, and discovering a purpose you have overlooked in the past"

~ Vince Lombardi, Jr. ~

In our last chapter, we talked about a 5-step process to discover your life purpose. In this chapter I'm going to unveil a 5-step process to discover your business purpose, so you know what kind of business to start and run.

But, before I do, it's important that I also highlight my opinion and belief that everyone on planet earth is destined to one day own their business. There's a lot of reasons why I believe this to be true, but let's start with something we all desire in life: Success.

I love what John Maxwell has to say about success. For much of his early life, he viewed success as a destination. Some point in the not-too-distant future when we'd all wake up one day and pronounce to the world that we're a success and say see, "I made it!"

He said that viewpoint on success would lead to what he calls "destination disease," which is the belief that if we just arrive somewhere (as in attain a position, accomplish a goal, find our spouse), we would have met the definition of success.

However, he soon realized that was a very poor definition of success. Rather than a destination, he saw success as an ongoing process of growth, a journey and not a destination. That's led to him defining success as the combination of these three things:

- Knowing your purpose in life
- Growing to reach your maximum potential, and
- Sowing seeds that benefit others

As a Christian, I know that I was created in the image of Christ. The God that I believe in, and serve, is responsible for everything we see on planet earth. This is my belief and my Bible tells me that God the Father is the creator of everything that has ever existed.

As a father of 3 amazing kids, I know that one of the greatest compliments I can receive is for someone to tell me that my kids are just like me. I hear it all the time when people see our family pictures or members of my family notice some of the things our kids do.

If I was created in the image of the Creator himself, then one of the biggest compliments I can give my Spiritual Father is to be perpetually "caught" in the act of creating. The ability to have unfiltered and uninhibited expression of our innate creativity is one of God's greatest gifts to us.

As an employee for someone else, I believe that your innate gift to give full expression to your creativity can be, and usually is, stifled, if not altogether limited. I know for me personally, I always felt like 'a fish out of water' in Corporate America because of the leadership traits God placed within me to challenge conventional wisdom.

Again, you don't have to hold the same beliefs I hold, but from my personal experience and my study of some of the most successful people on earth, they all seem to have found their path to entrepreneurship, where they gave full and uninhibited expression to their creativity.

Look no further than how Jeff Bezos transformed the retail industry, how Mark Zuckerberg has transformed our online social experiences, or how Elon Musk has transformed the automotive industry with the commercialization of electric vehicles.

The list is long and plenty of billionaires who've transformed our way of life by giving full expression to their innate creativity. Don't get me wrong, you can have a great life as an employee. I just believe entrepreneurs have the ability to live an extraordinary life.

And, should you ever be bold enough to leap into the adventure of entrepreneurship, I think it would be great to know which business to start and run. I'm talking about the kind of business that allows you to live life on our own terms, the kind of business you and your spouse could run from the comfort of your own home, the local library, or even the beach.

To answer the question of which kind of business you should start and run, we have to start with this core fundamental model I'm about to share with you below:

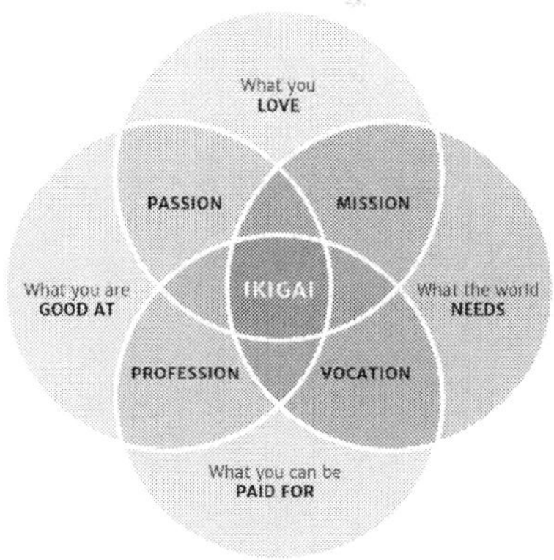

This model comes from the Japanese word Ikigai (ee-key-guy). Even though the word is spelled with the letter "I," it's pronounced (ee-key-guy) and it literally means "Your Reason For Being."

And, it's the intersection of four specific things:

1. Doing what you love. You see that in the middle of the yellow circle
2. On the right...it's Doing what the world needs
3. On the left...it's Doing what you're good at
4. And at the bottom...it's Doing what you can be paid for

So, it's the intersection of what you love, what the world needs, what you can be paid for, and what you're good at.

A few things to note here is that when you think about what the world needs, it's not the whole world we're talking about. We're just referring to that part of the world that you interact with, that you impact at some level.

And, as for what you think you can be paid for, that's really about what "they" value. I mean just because you think they value something, if you bring it to the world and they're like, well, I don't really care about that, then you're not really going to get paid for it. If you've ever watched an episode of Shark Tank, you've seen this play out many times, right?

And then as it relates to the overlapping of the circles, here's what you should be aware of:

1. If you love it and the world needs it, then there's your mission
2. If the world needs it and you can be paid for it, there's your vocation
3. If you're really good at it and you can be paid for it, there's your profession
4. And if you love it and are good at it, that's your passion

But it's that perfect combination in the middle called "IKIGAI" that we want you to seek and explore.

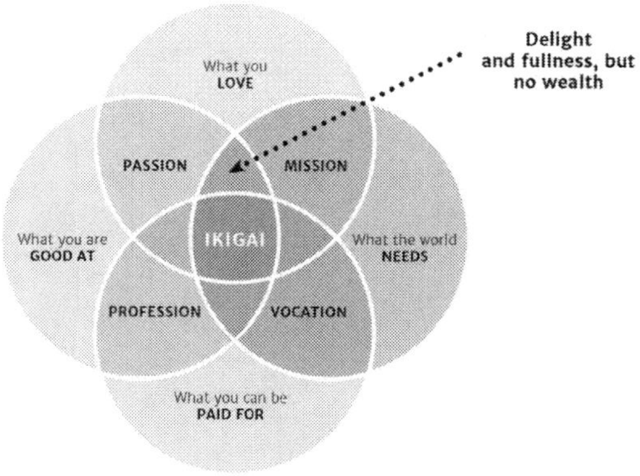

Because here's what happens. If you have the top 3 in the example above but can't be paid for it. In other words, you're good at it, you love it and the world needs it, but you can't really get a lot of money from it, then you have delight and fullness, but you don't have any wealth.

Now, if you're already financially wealthy, if you're already financially independent, then it doesn't matter, right? Only these 3 things are going to matter to you in what you do in business and if the 4th one is there, then great, you have more financial resources to donate to causes you care about or whatever. Does that make sense?

But, the problem is that most of us, most baby boomers, most Gen X'rs, and certainly Gen Y and Gen Z, still need to get paid for what they are doing, to have the most impact and to have the most amount of scale possible.

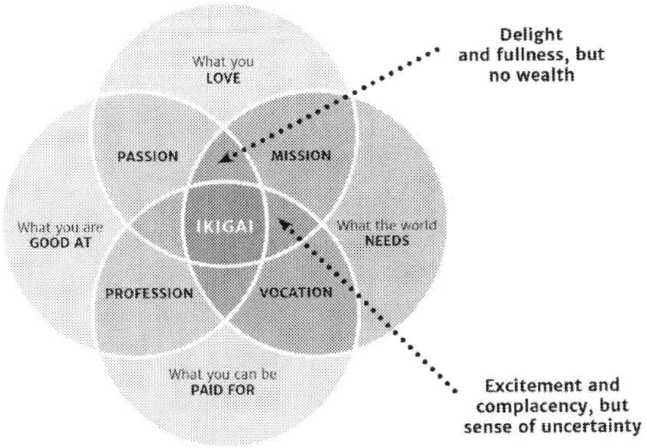

Now if you love it, the world needs it, and you can be paid for it, then as you see above, what you have is excitement and complacency, but a growing sense of uncertainty, because you're not really good at it, and you're not sure you're really able to have longevity with what you're doing.

A lot of people starting a business for the first time may find themselves in this category, where they are embarking on doing something they love, they know the world needs it, they know they can be paid for it, but they're uncertain they're really good at it, yet.

The next one, as pictured at the bottom of the prior page, is if you're good at it, you can be paid for it and the world needs it, but you don't necessarily love it. Here you're comfortable, but there's a feeling of emptiness. And, I'll give you an example from my life.

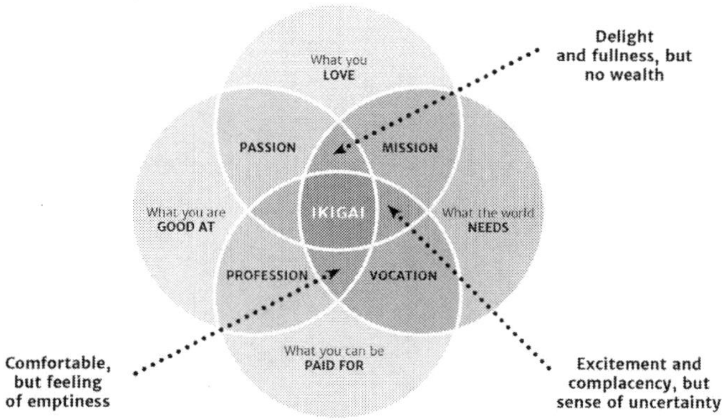

I got a degree in Accounting in 1996, I've been a CPA since 1998. I'm good at what CPAs do, I can get paid for it and the world needs it, but I don't really love it. I don't love being stuck in numbers all day, I don't love the long hours during tax season. There's a lot I don't love about the profession, yet I'm good at it, can get paid for it, and the world needs it.

Because I don't love it, I don't market those services, I don't run a traditional CPA firm. Instead, I gravitate more towards financial, consulting and coaching services over the years and I don't do any accounting work anymore and I don't operate a "tax return mill" where I'm cranking out hundreds of tax returns during tax season. I can do the work, but I don't love it because it doesn't satisfy me at the core of who I am, like say speaking, consulting and coaching does.

And, I'm not alone in the pool of people who do work they are good at, get paid for and the world needs it. Just a day after Labor Day this year (2021), I shared a post on social media in which I noted that a recent Gallup poll showed that 85% of the global working population wasn't engaged at their work.

Translated another way, that means that 85% of our global workforce doesn't absolutely love their work. If you check within your circles of influence, you might find that statistic to be fairly accurate, and it's just sad to be honest with you.

So, if you are going to start or launch a business, we don't want you to have a business like that. It's absolutely the worst combination out of all 4 of these circles to have. If you make money at a business you don't love, you're trapped. It's worse than losing money in a business.

I've made and lost 7 figures twice in my life and as painful as those were, the one thing I know is that within a business where you're losing money, you can change, modify and grow. But if you're stuck because you're in a business where you're making money, but you don't love what you do, sometimes you're stuck there for years and honestly, that can be very depressing.

Thankfully, it only took me 4 years in public accounting to realize that's not what I wanted to do long term, then I did 2 years in financial services and realized I didn't want to be an employee anymore...actually I was forced into becoming an entrepreneur because God knew I wouldn't 'launch out' on my own accord.

But, in looking back at what's now been almost two decades of being an entrepreneur, it's been one of the best decisions I've ever made. I tell people I meet that "I'm certifiably unemployable."

There's no amount of money in the world that could make me go back to being an employee for someone else or doing accounting work full time. It's just not what I love, it's not what makes me come alive.

For years, I've seen people stuck in a job or a business, because they're making money at it, but it's not what they love. That's not a great place to be and we don't want that happening to you.

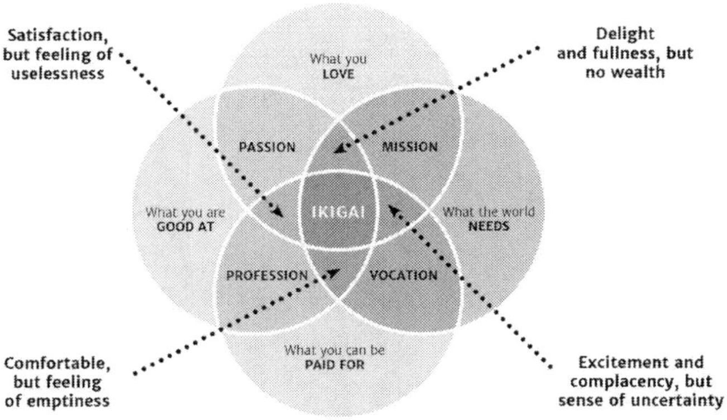

And, the 4th one is everything except what the world needs. So you love it, you're good at it, and you can be paid for it. In this case, there's satisfaction from what you're doing for sure. But, it's a bit of a feeling of uselessness, because you're not really sure if this is really making a difference, especially if the world doesn't need it.

Sometimes, I see this with 'wannabe entrepreneurs' masking as inventors. They want all this free advice from you, yet when you ask them about what they're doing, they want you to sign all of these non-disclosure agreements, and yet want to get all this free advice at the same time, instead of paying my hourly consulting rate for my time. Very frustrating at times...but I digress. Maybe I'm the only one who has a problem with that or who deals with it sometimes with people who have these wild ideas of what they want to do without any real demonstrated market potential.

Which is why I love the work of some of my mentors, people I've worked with like Ryan Levesque, founder of the 'Ask Method,' which allows you to know ahead of time what a market needs. Then there's Tom Matzen, who does 'Validation Calls' before rolling out a High Ticket offer. That way, you're not spending all this time, and effort, going to market, with a product or solution, that the market does not need.

If you have ever launched an idea you thought was great, only to realize the market didn't really need it or want it, then chances are this resonates with you. You likely have a greater appreciation for the importance of proving there's a market for your product and services, before actually going to market with them.

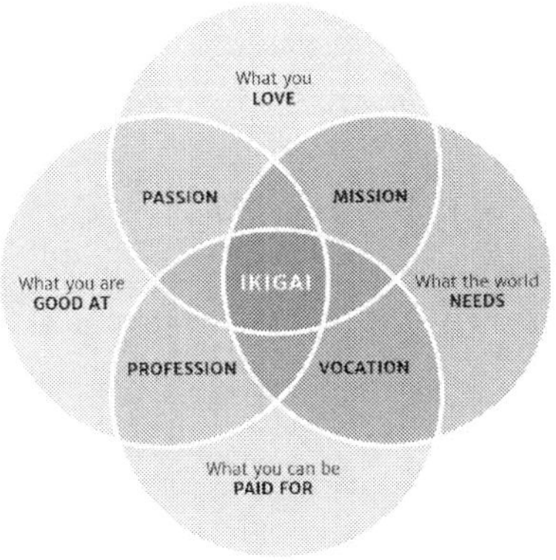

So, the key is to find what works in the middle of all 4 of these circles, which we call IKIGAI.

So, here's how we summarize this:

1. What do you love to do?
2. What are you good at?
3. What does the world need?
4. What can you be paid for?
5. What's at the intersection of all 4 questions above?

The way to practically go about doing this is rather simple. You don't want to start making a list of everything that fits into all 4 circles. Instead, you want to focus your time, and attention, on the first two.

So, start by making two separate lists. One with all the things you love to do, and the other, with all the things you're good at. Don't try to combine them right away. I find it's easier to make a list of all the things you love to do first.

Then, make a list of all the things that you're good at. Doing it this way will get you a more comprehensive, and in depth look at this. Then, you can start finding the intersection of what you love to do, and what you're good at.

Then, you can add in what the world needs, and what you can be paid for, which will ultimately lead you to your final destination: "IKIGAI."

We have come to the conclusion of part 1 of this book, where we contemplated: Why Purpose Is Key To Being Wealthy. As we contemplated that idea, we explored why early retirement should not be your purpose in chapter 1.

In chapter 2, we clarified who this book and message is really for. Acknowledging the importance of knowing your why was discussed in chapter 3.

Then, a 5 step process to discover your life purpose was analyzed in chapter 4. Finally, we concluded with a look at a 5 step process to discover your business purpose in this 5th chapter.

In part 2 of this book, we'll take 5 chapters to explore how to accelerate the creation of wealth. And, in the next chapter, I'll discuss finding a high income earning opportunity as your first step.

But first, here are a few chapter reflection questions for you.

FOR REFLECTION:

1. If you could be the architect of your life and you could redesign it, what are the things that interest you? What do you love to do?
2. Make a list of all of your abilities. This list should include things that you are naturally good at, things that you maybe even take for granted,

but others wish they could do.

3. As you look at the world in which we live in today, what are some of the biggest problems that remain unsolved in the various industries and niches that people work in. What exactly do you think the world needs right now?
4. What can you do that celebrates your unique giftedness in solving a problem that people are willing to generously compensate you for? What can you get paid for?
5. Reflect on your responses to questions 1 - 4 above, and see if you can identify what lies at the intersection of your responses to all four of the questions you just answered?

PART 2

How To **Accelerate The Creation** Of Wealth

CHAPTER 6

Finding A High Income Earning Opportunity

"Actions are purposeful, and are taken in pursuit of goals to achieve a defined end"

~ Barry Linetsky ~

Over the first part of this book, I've provided a hearty discussion of why purpose is key to being wealthy. And, if you're convinced that early retirement shouldn't be your purpose, and you know the message of this book is starting to resonate with you, then you are clear on the importance of knowing your WHY.

You now have a 5 step process you can use to discover your life and your business purpose. Perhaps, you have an idea of which business you should start and run. As you explore ideas around this topic, let's be aware that if our goal is to create wealth, and lots of it, then not any ole' business will do.

We want to engage in a business that has the highest probability of success. We want one that will provide us with the highest income earning opportunity possible. The quickest way to get to that point, is to understand that the only reason a business exists, is to solve a problem.

And, when it comes to solving problems as a business owner, the 5 biggest problems you can solve are also coincidentally the 5 biggest reasons a customer ever buys from you. Recognizing what these 5 reasons are, and designing a business to address them, will also position you to experience the highest income earning opportunity possible, through your business.

The 5 biggest reasons a customer ever buys from you are to:

1. Make money
2. Save money
3. Stay out of jail
4. Have a better life; or
5. Have better relationships

If you want to buy, start, or run a business that's going to be successful, you better focus on at least one of those reasons listed above. If you can build a business that addresses all 5, then it's very likely that you'll have an unfair advantage over others. After discovering my WHY and having clarity on my life and business purpose, I responded to the divine inspiration from God to launch the Righteous Billionaire Movement and design my Manifest Wealth Safely Program.

Truth be told, it wasn't until I sat down to write this book that I realized God had given me an unfair advantage with the way my program is designed, and what we do within the Movement. Allow me to share some relevant information about both, to further illustrate this.

The top 10 reasons why you, and others, are attracted to the Righteous Billionaire Movement are because you're interested in:

1. Shrinking your financial independence timeline down from 30 years to as little as 2 to 5 years.
2. Finding a solution to the inept leadership we find in our nation and in most nations today.
3. Being the solution to that inept leadership by raising your "leadership lid" circa John Maxwell's teachings and those of other great leaders of our time.

4. Not just retiring early, but being refired about your purpose to change the world.
5. Awakening from the drunken stupor of mediocrity and making moves in this life that are extraordinary.
6. Leveraging the secrets of top-tier financial institutions and family offices to manifest wealth safely and quickly, so you can enjoy six and seven figure streams of passive income.
7. Creating a legacy of positive changes in your nation and community.
8. Identifying, clarifying, and magnifying your purpose.
9. Raising your leadership capital, and becoming a next generation leader, who changed the world, and who brings an end to most of the wickedness, and evil, that's present today.
10. Becoming a Billionaire before the year 2030 and using both your financial and leadership capital to reinstitute righteousness at the foundation of all nations.

When you join our movement and/or participate in our Manifest Wealth Safely Program, you get exposed to the right financial opportunities, as well as the mentoring and coaching that's geared at making you a master of the seven realms of wealth, which are:

» Spiritual: deals with how wealthy your relationship is with the creator of the universe.
» Soulful: looks at how wealthy your mind, will, and emotions are, based on what you're feeding it.
» Physical: recognizes that there is no real wealth to be enjoyed without one's physical health.
» Relational: looks at how wealthy your relationships are with those you love.
» Influential: examines how wealthy you are in your ability to influence others decisions.
» Social: governs how wealthy you are in making your community better.
» Financial: ensures that you are a reservoir which currency abun-

dantly flows through.

Within the Righteous Billionaire Movement are 3 important pillars namely:

1. **Entrepreneurship:** to allow full expression of your creativity and allow you to find a high income earning opportunity.
2. **Leadership:** to raise up next generation leaders, whose leadership skills are as effective at home as they are out in the marketplace and their communities.
3. **Wealth Creation:** to produce, protect and perpetuate billions of dollars of new wealth, that will be used to make purpose-driven, and legacy impacting, changes in the nations.

And, when I'm asked what I do, I share my unique value proposition with people by telling them that I help my clients manifest wealth safely and earn 1% to 25% monthly returns so they can pursue purpose-driven passion projects they love that can change the world.

What I've found is due to the curve balls of life, many of these 40 and 50-something year old business owners and working professionals feel like they are behind the 8-ball when it comes to securing their financial future. So, through my proprietary process, I show them how we can shrink 30-year financial independence timelines down to as little as 2 years.

Bottom line is I help my clients add at least $1,000,000 in new wealth and $100,000 in passive and sometimes tax-free income, in as little as 2 to 5 years, guaranteed. Now, I want to revisit how I've gained an unfair advantage with my business by addressing all 5 major reasons customers buy from a business. As a reminder, those 5 reasons are to:

1. **Make money** - the wealth and entrepreneurial pillar within my program addresses this.
2. **Save money** - the wealth and entrepreneurial pillar within my program addresses this.

3. **Stay out of jail** - the legal strategies to create tax-free income within my wealth pillar address this as does the leadership pillar.
4. **Have a better life** - the mentoring and coaching geared at making you a master of the seven realms of wealth does this.
5. **Have better relationships** - the mentoring and coaching geared at making you a master of the seven realms of wealth does this.

In a million years, I couldn't have come up with something like this on my own. Through the power of discovering my WHY and unlocking my life and business purpose, I gained an unfair advantage over my competition. Now I earn a high income by solving critically important problems for the clients I work with.

So, now that you know what finding a high income earning opportunity can look like when done properly, I want to provide some insights into the high income earning opportunity that my clients are taking advantage of, within the entrepreneurial pillar of my movement and programs.

I realize that you have many opportunities to consider in your pursuit of a high income earning opportunity as an entrepreneur, so I figured I'd share the one we have in our programs for your thoughts and consideration.

Entrepreneurship Isn't For The Faint At Heart

Before sharing the entrepreneurship opportunity my clients are participating in, it's important that I be totally honest with you, and tell you that this entrepreneurship journey isn't easy. Fact is that 62.8% of most entrepreneurs fail in their first 6 years, and those numbers are even higher in the coaching and consulting industry that my clients are participating in.

And, while the average client is worth as much as $60,000 a year in revenue to the coaches in my Seven Figure Mentor Program, a recent study by the International Coaching Federation, noted the global average annual income for a coach, is a whopping $51,000 a year, and that's in an industry that's set to exceed $300 billion in 2025.

I find that $51,000 number to be rather sad, especially when we have coaches in our program that can make that much, off just one client for the year. So, what gives? Why do so many entrepreneurs, coaches, and consultants struggle to be successful?

If we are being honest, there are many reasons. But, chief among them, is the fact that most entrepreneurs are just wearing too many hats. Unless you're already doing millions of dollars in revenues each year, you are likely the Business Strategist, HR Manager, Graphics Designer, Web Analyst, Sales person, CFO, and CEO.

We joke about entrepreneurs wearing too many hats like it's a good thing. But, is it any wonder why so many of them fail when they are burdened with so many competing responsibilities?

So, when I thought about providing an entrepreneurial opportunity to the clients in my program, I first asked myself: Who are the best kind of clients to have? As I looked back at my varied experiences as a Certified Public Accountant, a Financial and Investment Advisor, a Speaker, Coach, and Consultant, it became really easy to narrow down who the best clients to serve in an entrepreneurial activity are. I won't keep you in suspense. It's business owners!

But, not just any business owner, I find those in that $500,000 to $3,000,000 space to be some of the best business owners to serve. These are people who are desperate for the right solutions to allow their companies to take the next quantum leap of growth and success they desire. And, when you can offer a solution that does exactly that, you have a very captive audience to the solutions you offer.

Do you remember the 5 big reasons any customer would ever buy from you? I managed to nail down 4 of the 5 in the entrepreneurial opportunity we offer to the clients in our Seven Figure Mentor Program (7FMP).

Our Seven Figure Mentor Program offers a turn-key business coaching solution that takes aspiring and existing coaches and consultants, and turns them into Seven Figure Mentors, who help business owners add more revenue and profits to their business, while improving their life, and enjoying better relationships with those they care about.

By the time our clients are done with the extensive training we offer them, they are able to articulate, illustrate, and demonstrate how they can help any business owner add up to $500,000 or more in new revenues, and profits to their business, over the next 12 months, and even guarantee it.

In the words of marketing genius Jay Abraham, that strong a unique value proposition goes a long way in establishing your strategy of preeminence in the marketplace, where you essentially become a category of one in the eyes of prospective clients you want to serve, and your competition becomes irrelevant in their minds.

Now, if you think that's a strong value proposition our coaches and consultants are offering to the business owner clients they serve, consider the value proposition we use in attracting clients into this entrepreneurial opportunity we offer.

For those who qualify to work with us, here's what our value proposition is: Give us two years, and we'll help you turn your annual income into a monthly income, while building a Seven-Figure Business Coaching Practice, that allows you to enjoy 12 weeks OFF a year, Guaranteed,...even if you know nothing about sales, marketing, or technology.

For every client where our coaches help these small business owners add $500,000 in new revenues and profits, that engagement is worth at least $60,000 in annual revenues to them. And, at that rate, you can see that it does not take many clients to build a thriving Seven Figure Business Coaching Practice.

Achieving financial freedom is important to us, heck it's the very topic of this book, right? But, even more important than financial freedom, is time freedom. And that's why baked into our business model are strategies to ensure our coaching clients can enjoy 12 weeks OFF each year, so that through our entrepreneurial opportunity we offer, they not only get to make and save more money, but they also get to have a better life, and enjoy better relationships with their family, and those they care about.

Did you notice how we hit 4 out of the 5 critical reasons a customer ever buys from you with the entrepreneurial opportunity we offer our coaches and consultants? Well, they also do the same for the business owner clients they serve within our Seven Figure Mentor Program.

As you explore which entrepreneurial options might be a good fit for you to find a high income earning opportunity, you want to make sure you select one that provides as many of those 5 critical reasons a customer ever buys from you. Doing so will virtually guarantee your success.

If you are wondering if the entrepreneurial opportunity we offer in our Seven Figure Mentor Program could be a good fit for you to land a high income earning opportunity, I'd ask that you ask yourself what you would be willing to do if you could:

» Be trained on a system that helps business owners discover how to generate more leads for their business, convert more of those leads to paying clients, increase the frequency with which those clients made purchases from the business, increase prices in a way where customers thank them for doing so, and rapidly increase profits?

» Master this system even if you know absolutely nothing about sales, marketing, accounting, finance or technology? We've developed a system of serving business owners in that $500,000 to $3,000,000 space that is so simple and effective, it's foolproof. And, even a 5 year old could do it.

» Be branded and positioned as an expert in the field of business growth services and as the only solution these business owners need for their pressing problem? Be seen as the one holding an oxygen tank to give them the air they need to breathe in business?

» Earn more money with one client than many make in an entire year, while delivering incredible value to the business owners you serve?

» Have a high income earning opportunity and be in business for yourself, but not by yourself?

» Learn and apply a new skill set that places you in the top 1% of all income earners, while affording you an incredible lifestyle, as you enjoy 12 weeks off each and every year?

» Generate raving fans and become a true authority with your work?

» Never have to worry about marketing again as you have your very own 100% completely customized and totally done for you lead creation factory, that, like a General Motors factory, consistently delivers at least 10 guaranteed leads and appointments each month, for you to monetize your unique value proposition to business owners in that $500,000 to $3,000,000 space?

» Create a high-revenue, high-margin, high-impact business coaching practice that's enrolling clients and cash flow positive within your first 90 days?

» Have full support to maximize each part of your business until it generates $1,000,000, guaranteed?

If these kinds of outcomes are what you desire when you embark on the journey of finding a high income earning opportunity as your first step to accelerate the creation of wealth, then the single most important action you can take right now, is to book a strategy session with me or a member of my team, to see if you are a good fit for our Seven Figure Mentor Program.

With the level of guarantees we offer, that include our viable program guarantee, ten leads per month guarantee, one million dollar program guarantee and our no strings attached ongoing support guarantee, I can assure you that we reject more applicants than we accept in the program.

However, you'll be pleased to know that it costs you nothing to apply, to see if you qualify for the program. The first step in the qualification process is to book a call at the link below.

Scheduling link: **http://call.sevenfigurementorprogram.com**

In the introduction to this book, I said that, with as complex a subject matter as I'm tackling with the title of this book, the entirety of this book can be summed up in two three step plans: one three for those who have $100,000 in liquid net worth and one for those who don't.

Steps 2 and 3 are similar for both groups. If you already have $100,000 in liquid net worth, my assumption, though not necessarily always correct, was that perhaps you already have a high income earning opportunity, and so step 1 for you was to Discover Your Purpose.

For those who don't have $100,000 in liquid net worth, this chapter covers what you need to know about your step 1, which is to Find A High Income Earning Opportunity. Having excess income to put powerfully to work for you, is the first step to accelerate the creation of wealth. I hope you've found what I shared in this chapter to be valuable to your cause.

In the next chapter, I'll explore the next step to accelerate the creation of wealth, which is to Avoid The Mom and Dad Plan. But first, here are a few chapter reflection questions for you.

FOR REFLECTION:

1. Are you convinced that entrepreneurship is the fastest path to a high income earning opportunity?
2. How many of the 5 big reasons why customers buy can you include in your entrepreneurial idea?
3. Does your business idea serve the needs of the most desirable clients, which just happens to be small business owners?
4. Are you open to guaranteeing the results you provide with your business idea?
5. Could you see yourself as a coach, consultant, or mentor to small business owners?

CHAPTER 7

Avoid The "Mom and Dad Plan"

"Rather than love, than money, than fame,
give me truth"

~ Henry David Thoreau ~

In the 1992 movie, A Few Good Men, there's an iconic moment where Lieutenant Kaffe, played by Tom Cruise, asks Colonel Jessep, a character played by Jack Nicholson, an all too important question that's at the center of the plot of the movie. The question asked was: "Did you order the Code Red?!"

And, while the Judge at the hearing tells the Colonel he doesn't have to answer the question, he proceeds to say "I'll answer the question." Then, he looks at the Lieutenant, and says, "You want answers?" almost sarcastically, to which the Lieutenant says, "I think I'm entitled to them."

Almost like a Texas standoff, the Colonel stares at the Lieutenant and says, "You want answers?", to which the Lieutenant replies, "I want the truth!" And, it's then, we hear the iconic line that has stood with us for ages, as the Colonel replies: "You can't handle the truth!"

I'm afraid that, with what I'm about to share with you, in all likelihood, you probably can't handle the truth. But like a moral obligation, I feel compelled to share this truth with you. Are you ready for it? Are you really ready for it?

All right, here we go: You've been lied to! By the Democrats, the Republicans, and the Government? Yes, we know all three are capable of bending the truth. But, the person who's lied to you, is even more personal. It's MOM and DAD... your parents. Hard to believe?, I know.

But…

If your parents were like mine or most parents, they probably told you to go to school, work hard and get a good job, and deemed that as the formula and path to success in life. So, you got A's in school and went to work for someone only to find out that…

The A students in school are the ones who end up working for the C students (nod to Robert Kiyosaki here). And it's the C students, those who own businesses, who realize that hiring those A students from school is actually good for business.

Don't believe me? Read up on most of the successful billionaires out there and you'll find they weren't A students…many even dropped out of school.
Here's a short list of them that you might recognize:

1. Howard Hughes, the legendary businessman, investor, film producer, and philanthropist.
2. Ted Turner, businessman, media titan, and founder Turner Broadcast Network and CNN.
3. Mickey Arison, businessman ,and owner of Carnival Cruise Line and the Miami Heat.
4. Steve Jobs, businessman, technology icon, and founder of Apple.
5. Bill Gates, businessman, philanthropist, and founder of Microsoft.
6. Mark Zuckerberg, businessman, philanthropist, and founder of Facebook.
7. John D. Rockefeller, businessman, and oil refinery titan, who's name is synonymous with "rich."

Did you notice a common thread with this short list of billionaires, beyond the fact that they all dropped out of college? It's the fact that they were all businessmen which further reinforces the idea of discovering your business purpose and finding a high income earning opportunity as an entrepreneur.

You should also notice the themes of purpose, and high-income earning opportunity, as the first step in the three-step process I outline in the introduction of this book, one plan summarizing the truth contained in this book for those who have $100,000 in liquid net worth and one plan for those who don't.

What is the Mom and Dad Plan?

The Mom and Dad Plan is a system of personal money management that you've been taught to follow and accept since you were a child. We've all been on this same basic plan for generations now, and while it might have worked wonders for your grandparents, the trouble today is it doesn't work for you.

People follow the Mom and Dad Plan with the expectation of building financial security as they approach retirement. However, the sheer mechanics of how the Mom and Dad Plan works strips these same people of the financial security they expected as retirement approaches.

Let's face it, without even going into the specifics of everything that's wrong with the Mom and Dad Plan, something I do in much more detail in my E-book: ***6 Shortcomings Of The Mom And Dad Plan and 3 Simple Steps To Regain Financial Security***, which as a purchaser of this book, you will find how to gain access to it in the ***How To Get More Help*** section of this book, all we have to do is look at what's happening in our present day, to see that we are in big financial trouble!

As a country, nation, and even globally, we are in the middle of one of the biggest financial crises since the great depression. Don't let the gains you've seen in the stock market since its last major crash of 2008 fool you.

Newsflash = > We are in the middle of a bubble that's waiting to burst!
The folks in Washington can't seem to balance our budget. As each year passes, our national debt continues to rise like a runaway freight train. And, with a social security crisis looming, wars we've been financing on credit cards piling up, and new policies and initiatives to curb the economic fallout from the pandemic of 2020 increasing at an alarming rate, our governments only solution, thus far, has been to print more money.

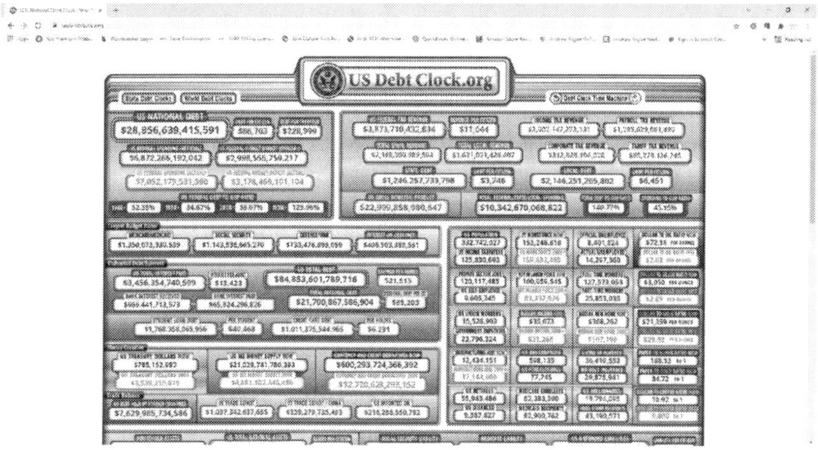

You don't have to possess a Harvard degree to be able to read two simple numbers from the US Debt Clock.org website screenshot above, to recognize how dire our situation is. Those two numbers are: US Federal tax revenues at $3,873,710,432,834 compared to US Federal Spending (Actual) of $7,052,179,531,590.

Now, any way you slice it, those are some pretty big numbers to contend with. So, let's break this down to numbers that are a little easier to wrap our minds around. If you are spending $2 for every $1 you bring in as income, how sustainable is that?

If you said "not very", you're absolutely right! And, while our national debt is at over $28 Trillion dollars and soon to eclipse $30 Trillion, how does that number compare to our US Gross Domestic Product of about $22.9 Trillion. It's almost 50% higher, right?

At almost $30 Trillion in national debt as of the fourth quarter of 2021, it's important to note that just 10 years ago in 2011, our national debt was just $14.79 Trillion. So, in 10 years, we've seen our national debt essentially double, and we are yet to see a corresponding deterioration in our economy? For a deeper look into some of the factors that have impacted the rise of our national debt, check out this page below for a cumulative look at this from 1929 to 2020: **https://www.thebalance.com/national-debt-by-year-compared-to-gdp-and-major-events-3306287**

Did I mention that 2008 was the last major correction the stock market saw? Have you noticed how in the fourth quarter of 2021, real estate properties are at all time highs, with an insatiable sellers market, in which sellers can list a property for $400,000, but the pent up demand for real estate, result in a bidding war from buyers, and a final sale of the property at $450,000?

Did you hear about the shortage of technology chips, car parts, groceries and other basic staples that have driven up the prices of everything from used cars, homes, groceries, and essentially anything you can spend your currency on here towards the end of 2021?

Less I digress too far from the topic of this chapter, my point for you is to recognize the pending perils that lie ahead for our nation as well as to understand how a lot of what we've learned from our well-meaning mom and dad, about our personal finances may be the very thing that prevents us from accelerating the creation of wealth, and instead, puts us in financial hurt.

You've heard of late-night host David Letterman's Top 10 Lists. Well, here are Ike's Top 7, the top 7 signs that the Mom and Dad Plan is leading you to financial ruin:

1. You believe that earning average returns is the pathway to investment success. Nothing could be further from the truth in Wall Street where a mutual fund could have an average 20% rate of return for 2 years, even though you lost money in that same period of time.

2. You believe that working with investment brokers, like your mom and dad did is your best path to achieve financial success. Whether you listen to Warren Buffet or Arthur Levitt, the former SEC Chairman, or you listen to me, a former Investment Advisor, they and I will tell you that investment brokers don't have your best interest at heart. By nature of the competing interests between the broker, their brokerage firm and you the client, it's virtually impossible for them to. A broker is mandated to sell the brokerage firm's products. The broker's compensation is penalized if they are not selling the brokerage firm's products, many of which may not truly be in the interest of you, the client.

3. Thinking you can pick winning stocks to achieve investment success. It's fool's gold, and you might have better odds at achieving financial success by gambling in Las Vegas.

4. Believing that the only way to be debt free is by eliminating all forms of debt. You must recognize that just as there's good and bad bacteria, there's also good and bad debt. Bad debt, you want to eliminate as quickly as possible. Good debt, on the other hand, can help you create significant wealth and achieve financial independence quickly. Let me ask you this question: If you had your choice of retiring with $2 million in liquid investable assets, and absolutely no debt, or retiring with $12 million in liquid investable assets and having $2 million in good debt, which would you rather have? I know what my choice would be!

5. Buying into the hype that your home is your biggest investment. If you still think so, ask all the folks who saw their housing values decline by 50% or more during the housing market crash of 2007 and 2008. Ask anyone who thinks their house is their biggest investment how much income that house was providing to them during the crash, or now for that matter? Not only is your house not your biggest investment, it's actually one of the most risky investments you might have. I discuss this topic in much more detail in my book that's available on Amazon,

Winning The Money Game: Separating The Myths From The Truth - Everything You Don't Know About Achieving Financial Independence.

6. Believing you are more secure having your house paid off than financed 100%. This financial "myth" goes back to the early 1900's when banks could foreclose on your home even if you were making timely payments on your home. Since about the 1950's, that law has not been on the books. The only way a bank can foreclose on your home today is if you are delinquent on your payments. So, if your house should not be your biggest investment, why would you want to have all your money tied up in your house, sitting there, doing nothing but waiting for the next housing crash to wipe out 50% of its value? If taking money, sticking it in a tin can, and burying it in the back of your house, with the hopes that it will still be there, and worth the same value when you need it, doesn't seem like a wise idea, why would doing the same with all of "your money" you have sitting in your "paid-off" home be a wise decision?

7. You believe that you'll be in a lower tax bracket when you retire. With tax rates at historically low levels and a plethora of domestic and global economic issues weighing heavily on our country, the only place taxes are headed from where we are at, now at the end of 2021, is "up, up, up," as my toddler used to say when she wanted me to pick her up. Newsflash: If you accumulated much of your wealth in tax-deferred vehicles like 401K's and Traditional IRA's, thinking you would be at a lower tax bracket when you retire, I'm afraid to tell you that you're in for a very big shock. Just pay attention to what President Biden's administration is up to with taxation for a sign for where they are headed. Then, think of rocket ships to get a clue for where they are headed.

While the diagnosis of what the Mom and Dad Plan is doing to ruin your chances of attaining financial security is dire and gloomy, I want to assure you that no matter how deeply entrenched you might be in the Mom and Dad Plan, there is in fact hope for you. I tackle and eliminate the inherent problems of the Mom and Dad Plan in the Manifest Wealth + 6 Figure Roadmap we design for my clients in my Manifest Wealth Safely Program.

In the next chapter, I'll explore the next step to accelerate the creation of wealth, which is to: Beware Of The Perils Of The Financial Services Industry. But first, here are a few chapter reflection questions for you.

FOR REFLECTION:

1. How does knowing the truth about the Mom and Dad Plan make you feel?
2. If you aren't already one, does the idea of becoming an entrepreneur seem more or less appealing to you?
3. Why does becoming an entrepreneur seem more or less appealing for you?
4. If the data shared in this chapter hasn't convinced you that we are already in the middle of a financial crisis, what indicators should you be looking at to determine if we are?
5. What kind of impact would it have to your overall financial plan if when you retired, taxes were significantly higher then, than they are now?

CHAPTER 8

Beware Of The Perils Of The Financial Services Industry

"The truth will set you free, but first it will make you miserable"

~ James A. Garfield ~

Ever since I was a child, I've been fascinated by money. Growing up in Nigeria, I loved one of our family traditions. We'd spend Christmas at my Grandfather's compound aka "estate" in the Westernized world. At some point during our stay, all of the children would be summoned to his expansive living room that must have been like 3,000 square feet.

In his living room, our extended family would sit in chairs all around the circumference of the room. I'm talking mom, dad, uncles, aunts, cousins, nephews, the whole nine. The younger generation would then be asked to go through the room and share how well they did in school that year.

Getting a good education is a core foundation in my family and several members of my family have graduated from Ivy league schools in Great Britain and the United States. While it's been a good core value for my family, there are times when it's been almost to a fault.

As we would share how well we did for the school year, we would get rewarded with prizes (almost always money) from our parents, uncles, aunts and other older relatives. And, while my older siblings spent their cash winnings on clothes or toys, at the age of eight, I converted my dad's old briefcase into a makeshift bank and started saving my winnings.

So, even at the tender age of eight, I had figured out how to save my money, a lesson that has served me well in life. What I didn't figure out was how to stop the "robbers," in the form of my "older siblings," from breaking into my bank.

So, when I look at the career path I've taken that's included work as an Accountant, Tax Consultant, Financial Planner, Investment Advisor, Insurance Professional, Business Growth Strategist, Financial Coach, Money and Abundance Mindset Coach, to my most recent initiative with the launch of the Righteous Billionaire Movement and the work I do in my Manifest Wealth Safely Program, I can see how I was always destined to be doing the work I'm doing now within the Financial Services Industry.

So, it goes without saying that I love the Financial Services Industry. However, you don't have to be a fan of the late artist, Prince, to realize that you can have a love-hate relationship with that thing you love so much.

If you remember when I shared my WHY in Chapter 3, I said that part of my WHY is to Make Sense of the Complex and Challenging. I love taking things that are difficult and complex and solving them, to help other people understand them, so they make sense to them.

One of the things that I hate within the Financial Services Industry is the lack of transparency and the overt and covert attempts to really confuse the public they are supposed to be serving. Having held both an insurance license and investment advisors license, I can tell you that both sides of this industry are at war with each other, in an attempt to have the consuming public think that one side of the fence is better than the other.

It should never be a case that the products and solutions offered by the insurance industry are superior or better than those offered by the investment industry. Nor should it be the other way around. In my professional opinion, it's not so much a case of either/or, as it is a case of and (both). You should have both investment advisory solutions, as well as insurance industry solutions, to round out your overall financial plan, as they each have a place within your plan.

I could go on and on about many of the nuances of the industry that I take issue with, but that would take a whole volume, or even a series of books, to do so. Instead, what I'd like to do is share the truth about some of the perils of the industry that you should be aware of.

And, while this truth will set you free, at first, you might find that it makes you miserable. If that happens, it's OK. Awareness is the first step to making any significant changes in our life. We can't change what we are not aware of.

So, consider any discomfort you feel as I share this information a good thing. I will present eight distinct perils that I identify as problems. Then, rather than leave you hanging with just the problems, the good news is I'll offer up a solution for your consideration for each problem.

Here are the 8 perils of the Financial Services Industry that you should be aware of:

PERIL 1

1a. Problem: You work hard, following the traditional path of funding your 401K & IRA. A decade later, markets collapse, your account loses 50% and all that hard work is wiped out.

1b. Solution: Realize that a 50% loss requires a 100% gain just to breakeven. With 7% average annual returns, it takes 10 years to breakeven again. So, adopt alternative investing strategies to avoid this.

PERIL 2

2a. Problem: You've made investment decisions based on Wall Street's manipulated "average" returns, where a mutual fund could have an average 20% ROR for the 2 years you've owned it, even though you've lost money in that time.

2b. Solution: Identify options to earn "real" rates of return that aren't manipulated by Wall Street.

PERIL 3

3a. Problem: Because DALBAR reported the S & P 500 index has a 9.96% 30-year average annual Rate of Return (hereafter ROR) as of Dec. 31, 2019, you think you could do better on your own.

3b. Solution: Recognize that DALBAR's QAIB Report shows the average investor did 50% worse with a 5.04% average annual ROR over the same time. So, you get professional help.

PERIL 4

4a. Problem: You get professional help only to realize the S&P 500 out-performed hedge funds and large cap fund managers over the last 10 years.

4b. Solution: Follow Buffet's advice and invest in an S&P 500 Index Fund.

PERIL 5

5a. Problem: You invest in an S&P 500 Index Fund but realize that even if it averages 10% ROR per year, time isn't on your side anymore.

5b. Solution: Find alternative wealth creation opportunities that have outperformed the S&P 500, hedge funds, and other money managers by a long shot.

PERIL 6

6a. Problem: You learn about FOREX as an alternative investment with great return potential and no market manipulation, but realize 90% of participants lose money 90% of the time.

6b. Solution: Figure out what 10% of the institutional participants are doing to make money 90% of the time and do it.

PERIL 7

7a. Problem: You learn that participating in PRE-IPO (Facebook, Tesla) deals are some of the best ways to create wealth but realize you don't have access to such opportunities.

7b. Solution: Switch "networks" to gain access.

PERIL 8

8a. Problem: The work you do today is literally and figuratively killing you. You know this work does not represent the mark you are to leave in this world.

8b. Solution: Discover your spiritual, life, and business purpose.

All eight of the above items are real problems that I have seen with over 20 years working in and around the financial services industry, both as an employee for one of the largest financial brokerage firms, as well as on my own when I owned my own Registered Investment Advisory Firm. I am no longer an investment advisor. But, with my role as a financial coach to my clients, I bring decades of wisdom, experience, and proprietary solutions to serve my clients.

Want to discover how I'm solving these problems, while shrinking financial independence timelines from 30 years to as little as 2 years, so you can fulfill your purpose, while enjoying six figures in passive income, as you pursue purpose-driven passion projects you love that can change the world?

Then, I invite you to book a strategy session with myself or a member of my team. I have limited spots available for these calls, so if you'd like to secure a spot on me or a member of my team's calendar, do so here:

http://call.manifestwealthsafely.com

In the next chapter, I'll explore the next step to accelerate the creation of wealth which is to: Minimize The Impact Of Taxation. But first, here are a few chapter reflection questions for you.

FOR REFLECTION:

1. Did you experience losses to your investment accounts of as much as 50% during the tech bubble of 2000 or the market crash of 2008?
2. Regardless of how much you might have lost during the market crashes of 2000 and 2008, how did you feel about seeing years of work and accumulated wealth seemingly disappear into thin air?
3. If your investments were to lose 50% during the next market crash, how would that impact your goals of retiring or becoming financially independent? And, can you afford that much of a loss during the next market crash?
4. If you're unable to stomach as much as a 50% loss during the next market crash, what steps have you taken to mitigate that risk?
5. Which of the 8 perils and solutions listed in this chapter resonate with you the most, that you are willing to do something about it, by taking some sort of new action, other than what you are currently doing?

CHAPTER 9

Minimize The Impact Of Taxation

"There may be liberty and justice for all,
but there are tax breaks only for some"

~ Martin Sullivan ~

Quick question to start out our chapter: If what you thought to be true about taxation and the future of tax rates turned out not to be true, when would you want to know? Hopefully, the only answer to that question you have is, "As soon as possible!"

From around 2008 to 2014, I taught financial workshops for several years at local universities and colleges that attracted a wide range of people. Some owned their own businesses, while others were employees. The age of attendees at the workshop ranged from 40 to 60 years old.

During some point in the workshop, I would ask the attendees this question: "How many of you think tax rates are going up?" Invariably, all the hands of attendees would go up signaling they thought so.

Yet, when I asked how many of the attendees have the lion's share of their retirement savings in IRA's, 401(k)'s, or other employer sponsored retirement plans, something shocking would happen: Invariably, all their hands would go up again.

What that told me was there was a major disconnect between what people think about what the future of tax rates will look like, versus what they are actually doing about it. It's kind of like knowing there's a blade coming down to chop your head off and doing absolutely nothing about it. Not a smart move, dare I say.

As of March 31, 2021, the Investment Company Institute reports that $35.4 trillion is what is held in the US retirement market, which included employer sponsored retirement plans of public and private sector employers, individual retirement accounts, and annuities.

By any stretch of the imagination, that's a lot of money and a great pool from which a government that is suffering from insufficient tax revenues can tap into. As a matter of fact, in September of 2021, a Forbes article noted 7 ways the new tax bill could impact retirement planning, with examples of everything from limiting contributions, to forcing you to take distributions from your plan, so you can pay taxes earlier than you ordinarily were supposed to.

Without even getting into the impact some of the new proposed tax bills could have on your retirement nest egg, it's worth understanding what most qualified plans are and do.

What Do 401K And Other Qualified Plans Do?

If you are like most people planning for their retirement, you're probably making contributions to a "tax-deferred qualified plan" of some sort. And why not? Everybody assumes it's better to take a current "deduction" for contributions to your qualified plan, and defer payment of taxes until you retire, because you'll be in a lower tax bracket then, right?

Well, if what you thought to be true about the future of tax rates turned out not to be true, when would you want to know? Now, right? Well, here are a few reasons why future tax rates are certain to be higher, beyond the year 2021, and why you will most certainly pay more in taxes:

- Historically, tax rates have increased, not decreased.
- Our national debt of almost $30 trillion is way out of control as evidenced by the usdebtclock.org chart I showed you in chapter 7.
- Most experts on the subject believe that given the fiscal condition in our country, tax rates will be dramatically higher.
- We have 10,000 baby boomers leaving the workforce daily, so we are losing their former tax contributions to social security and medicare.
- There have been significant bailouts initiated by our government for COVID-19.
- Those COVID19 government bailouts have made it financially advantageous for some to stay unemployed, rather than go back to work.
- Tax revenues are needed to still fund the decades long war on terror, as well as fund our highly inefficient social security and healthcare systems.
- Most retirees have fewer deductions in their retirement years and as such find more of their income subject to tax.
- Since most people are following the "Mom and Dad Plan" to prepare for their financial future, you likely believe the only way to be debt free is if you've paid off your mortgage. And, if you've done so, you will likely eliminate one of your biggest tax write offs, the home mortgage interest deduction.
- With few exemptions available to retirees from benefits like having children you're raising around, you'll forgo deductions and credits you once benefited from while working.
- As you compare our $3.8 trillion in federal tax revenues to our $7 trillion actual federal spending (from chapter 7), it's evident that we are already "broke" and "bankrupt" as a country. The only way out of that is to increase tax revenues.

How Is It Possible To Pay $500,000 In Income Taxes On Just A $210,000 Retirement Account

From the many retirees I've consulted with on a better way to planning for their retirement, most curse the day they started making contributions to their IRA's, 401K's, SEP's and other qualified plans, because they now realize that the amount of tax they pay on the back end, is significantly greater than the tax they saved on the front end. And, what's frightening is that the higher taxation equation occurs without even taking into account the potential that tax rates could be higher in their retirement years than during their working years. Let's look at an example.

Example of how to pay $500,000 in income taxes on just a $210,000 account

Example 1 – Jack and Jill's Retirement Plan or Uncle Sam's?

Annual IRA/401K Contribution = $6,000 X 35 Years = $210,000 Total Contributions
Tax Bracket = 33.3%
Tax Savings: $6,000 X 33.3% = $2,000 X 35 Years = $70,000 Total Tax Savings
$6,000 Per Year Growing at 7.5% for 35 Years = $1,000,000

	$1,000,000	
	X 7.5%	
	$ 75,000	Retirement Portfolio Income
	X 33.3%	Tax Bracket
	$ 25,000	Annual Tax
Therefore:	$ 75,000	Supplemental Retirement Income
Creates:	$ 25,000	Potential Annual Tax
Results:	$ 50,000	Net Spendable Income
Furthermore:	$ 70,000	Total Tax Savings for 35 Years
Creates:	$ 75,000	Tax Paid During 1st 3 Years of Retirement
Results:	**$ 5,000**	Excess Taxes Paid by 3rd Year of Retirement
Or:	**$ 500,000**	Total Taxes Paid by 20th Year of Retirement

Jack and Jill "Do What Everybody Else Does" represents a husband and wife who failed to avoid the "Mom and Dad Plan." They started setting aside $3,000 per year into IRA's or 401K's when they were age 25. They thought this was a good idea because, together, they were saving $6,000 before taxes into their retirement accounts.

In a 33.3% marginal tax bracket (combined Federal and State), it really only required them to give up $4,000 of CASH because "Uncle Sam" was contributing the other $2,000 in tax savings. With a planned retirement age of 60, that meant saving $2,000 for 35 years for total tax savings of $70,000, on total contributions of $210,000 over the same period.

At retirement, Jack and Jill are thrilled because after having averaged a 7.5% annual return, their retirement nest egg has grown to $1 million. If Jack and Jill were to make earnings only withdrawals (so as not to deplete their $1 million nest egg), their annual retirement portfolio income would be $75,000, assuming they continued to average a 7.5% return.

With income from other sources bringing their total taxable income to $150,000 and the fact that their home is paid off and kids are out of the house, they find that they don't have a lot of deductions or exemptions to offset their income and hence reduce their taxes at retirement.

The result of this is that they find that they are still at a 33.3% combined Federal and State marginal tax bracket. Thus, the $75,000 of retirement portfolio income ends up being taxed at that same rate, which results in $25,000 of tax that's attributable to their retirement plan income.

Thus, their net spendable income from their retirement plan is $50,000. Within just 3 years after retiring, they will pay back to Uncle Sam every dollar (and then some) that they saved in taxes on their $6,000 annual contributions, made to their retirement plan, for those 35 years.

To make sure you're tracking with me, so in 3 years of retirement, they've paid $75,000 in taxes versus the $70,000 tax benefit they got from their contributions over 35 years. If they are alive for 20 years after retiring, they'll have paid the government a total of $500,000 in taxes, versus the $70,000 tax benefit they got from their contributions during those 35 years of funding.

Oh, and let's not forget the fact that their original $1 million retirement nest egg has still not been taxed at this point, since they are living off the annual earnings of $75,000. Just so you are aware, they stand to lose anywhere from 50% to as much as 90% of this $1 million account value, from future income and estate taxation, depending on the value of their estate at death.

Inconvenient Truth: You may end up paying more tax by putting money into your 401K or other qualified retirement plan account than you ever saved by funding it. The quote at the beginning of chapter 8 by James A. Garfield is worth mentioning here: "The truth will set you free, but first, it will make you miserable!"

What Should You Do About This Ticking Tax Time Bomb?

The first step to any meaningful change in life is awareness. And, it's safe to say that by now you should be aware of the ticking tax time bomb waiting to explode in your traditional retirement accounts, assuming tax rates stay the same when you retire. You already know that's likely not going to happen. In fact, this situation will be much worse with higher tax rates in the future. The question then becomes what should you do about it?

When I became financially independent at the age of 34 in 2008, not only had I accumulated over a Seven Figure Net Worth, but I also had Six Figures in passive income. One of the neat things about that was that the lion share of my passive income was also tax-free.

When it comes to creating tax free income, there are lots of ways to navigate that terrain. For one, I took advantage of a little known loophole in the tax code back in 2010 that allowed for you to convert traditional retirement plans to ROTH plans and defer paying the tax on conversion for two full tax years. Understanding the nuances of the tax code and other strategies, I came up with my proprietary ZERO-TAX ROTH CONVERSION STRATEGY, which allowed clients to pay ZERO in taxes from ROTH conversions and enjoy tax-free income for life.

Today the opportunities to enjoy tax-free income at retirement include:

» Municipal Bonds

- Traditional ROTH IRA and ROTH 401(K) Plans
- ROTH Conversions
- Ike's Proprietary ZERO-TAX ROTH CONVERSION STRATEGY
- Life Insurance Retirement Plans (LIRP's) - I've written extensively on this subject with articles of mine on Huffington Post. Additionally, my friend, David McKnight, author of The Power of Zero: How To Get To The 0% Tax Bracket And Transform Your Retirement has also written extensively on this strategy as well
- Certain kinds of Business Trusts
- Certain kinds of Charitable Trusts and Business Entity Structures

Case Study On Minimizing The Impact Of Taxation

One of the clients I'm working with presently, is the perfect example of a Jill "Do What Everybody Else Does." We'll call her Jill for the purposes of our discussion. Jill is 59 years old and works in management for a company and makes right at about $100,000 a year. Her husband, we'll call him Jack, just went on disability 3 years ago, but only got "qualified" a year or so ago to draw a small disability income check.

Jill's story is pretty typical to what I see with many clients I work with. She started saving when she was 18 years old and built up a nice nest egg in her employer sponsored 401K saving account. Then, the 2008 market crash hit and she lost 60% of her life savings just like that.

As if that wasn't bad enough, she also lost her job. Fortunately for her, she found a loophole that allowed her to borrow funds from her 401K account and access that remaining 40% to help her navigate those difficult times.

She borrowed the remaining money in her retirement plan with the intention of paying it back. Well, you know what they say about the best of intentions, right? She never followed through on that. Thankfully, over the years, and with a little cooperation from the stock market, she's built her 401K account at her new employer back up to about a $125,000 balance.

When she first started working with me, she felt like she was woefully behind the "8-Ball" in preparing for a secure financial future, and thought she might have to work the rest of her life to be secure, as well as to provide the kind of financial assistance her grandkids would need when they eventually and prematurely lose their mom due to a debilitating health issue.

Her situation seemed hopeless, or so she thought. That was, until I revealed the Manifest Wealth + 6 Figure Roadmap I'd put together for her. Using a combination of the strategies to enjoy tax-free income in this chapter and coupling that with what you'll learn in chapter 10 on the top 9 wealth growth models, chapter 11 on the 5 reasons we fail to achieve our financial goals, and chapter 12 on the 5 ways we guarantee our client's success, Jill and her family will have a very bright financial future in as little as 5 years.

Specifically, the roadmap we've put together will take her $125,000 fully taxable 401K plan balance and turn it into a tax-free wealth haven, that in 5 years will be worth about $5.3 million. At that point, she can comfortably take $500,000 a year in tax-free income and still see her account balance continue to grow. This plan ensures she not only retires ahead of plan at age 64, but that she enjoys six-figures in tax-free income, while she pursues her purpose-driven passion projects and creates the kind of financial legacy she wants to create for her children and grandchildren.

Want to discover how I'm helping clients minimize the impact of taxation while shrinking financial independence timelines from 30 years to as little as 2 to 5 years, so you can fulfill your purpose, while enjoying six figures in passive income, as you pursue purpose-driven passion projects you love that can change the world?

Then, I invite you to book a strategy session with myself or a member of my team. I have limited spots available for these calls so if you'd like to secure a spot on me or a member of my team's calendar, do so here: **http://call.manifestwealthsafely.com**

In the next chapter, I'll explore the final step to accelerate the creation of wealth which is to Utilize The Top 9 Wealth Growth Models. But first, here are a few chapter reflection questions for you.

FOR REFLECTION:

1. What are your thoughts on where you think tax rates will be in the future?
2. If you think tax rates will be higher, have you taken any steps to minimize their impact on your financial future?
3. What financial steps have you taken that are consistent with the "Mom and Dad Plan" and that you might want to consider changing?
4. As you reflect on your response to question #3 above, what changes to your current situation might be prudent for you to make?
5. Given what you now know, if you had the choice to take a deduction on contributions to your retirement plans and simply be taxed in the future, versus forgoing any tax deductions on those contributions and enjoying all of the growth on your retirement plans tax free, which seems like the more prudent choice to you and why?

CHAPTER 10

Utilize The Top 9 Wealth Growth Models

"Risk comes from not knowing what you're doing.
Only invest in 'simple businesses' that you understand.
Rule No 1 of investing: Never lose money. Rule No #2:
Don't forget rule No 1"

~ Warren Buffet ~

You've heard me share my story of how I've made and lost a Seven-Figure Net Worth twice in my life. Some of those losses stemmed from business betrayals, being naive, being greedy, and being victimized by Ponzi Schemes.

Regardless of all of the extenuating external circumstances that might have contributed to my losses, I take full responsibility for all of them. There are things I've learned from the school of "hard knocks" that a Masters Degree in Personal Financial Planning, a Bachelor's Degree in Accounting, and multiple professionals licenses as a CPA, CFP, Investment Advisor and Insurance Professional never taught me.

I don't regret any of my past losses. As a matter of fact, I celebrate and I'm thankful for them as they've helped shape who I am today, and taught me many valuable lessons. Chief among those lessons are the three sentences found in the quote to start off this chapter:

» Know what you're doing to eliminate the risk of investing.

- » Only invest in things that you understand.
- » Deploy strategic initiatives to help you never lose money in the long run. Sure, I'll take losses in the short term, because all investing involves a measure of risk and speculation, but those short term losses will always be abated by my strategic long term plan.

In the first four chapters of this second part of my book on how to accelerate the creation of wealth, we've explored strategies on how to find a high income earning opportunity, how to avoid the "mom and dad plan," how to avoid the perils of the financial services industry, and how to minimize the impact of taxation.

In this chapter, leaning into some of Warren Buffet's wisdom, I'm going to share with you my top 9 wealth growth models to help you accelerate the creation of wealth, so you can live an abundant life, and pursue purpose-driven passion projects you love, that can change the world. If you're like me and my clients, you know that there's more to life than what you've been currently experiencing. So, let's set the stage to help you live into that ideal life you've been dreaming of for years, and even provide you with some "Do It Yourself" (DIY) resources to help.

Growth Model #1: Private Lending To Real Estate Investors

You can diversify your portfolio by providing liquidity to major players in the real estate investing industry.

As a private money lender, you will loan money, secured by a note and mortgage/deed of trust, for the purpose of funding a real estate transaction.

Since the real estate investor is accessing capital from a non-institutional individual or company, they are willing to pay a higher rate of interest for access to your capital.

Potential Return: 10% to 20% for 90 to 180 days (project specific)

DIY Resource at https://www.privatefundingacademy.com

Personal Story

I've sat on both sides of the fence for private lending transactions. My first time was as a consumer and not as an investor. A lot of people marvel at the fact that I was able to purchase a home one month after I filed Chapter 7 Bankruptcy in 2003.

Part of the reason I was able to do so was because I understood the 'ins and outs' of real estate investing.

So, when it came time to buy a new home, we utilized some creative financing, and purchased our home using a Contract for Deed. The seller of our home "self-financed" our purchase, and we paid double digits in interest on our mortgage to him for 2 years.

This helped rebuild our credit, and in 2 years, we were able to refinance to single digits with a local bank.

Growth Model #2: Bridge Loans To Companies

You can diversify your portfolio by providing liquidity to emerging companies growing at a rapid pace.

As a private money lender, you will loan money, secured by a note and collateralized by real estate, for the purpose of funding a company's cash flow needs to fuel growth.

Since the corporation is accessing capital from a non-institutional individual or company, they are willing to pay a higher rate of interest for access to your capital.

Potential Return: 10% to 20% for 90 to 180 days (project specific)

DIY Resource at https://www.fundera.com/business-loans/guides/commercial-bridge-loans

Personal Story

My first 3 tranches of this in 2021 were:

95 day note at 18%
90 day note at 20%
90 day note at 21%

With money supply the way that it is right now, we are seeing notes in the high teens and early twenties. But historically, the interest rates on these notes are usually in the single digits to the 10% to 15% range.

The strategic partners I work with don't loan money to these corporations unless they post collateral in the form of real estate, that's 5 times the value of the loan, and also unencumbered by any existing liens.

Growth Model #3: Private Lending To Local Counties Via Tax Liens

You can diversify your portfolio by providing liquidity to your local county governments to continue providing services to local residents.

A tax lien is a legal claim against the property of an individual or business that fails to pay real estate taxes owed to the government. The lien reflects amount owed, penalties, plus statutory mandated interest and must be paid in 12 to 24 months or the owner risks loss of the property.

Buying the lien provides the opportunity to earn statutory interest rate over the period of time, or potentially own the property for pennies on the dollar, as a priority lien holder on the property.

Potential Return: 16% to 36% for 12 to 24 months (county specific)

DIY Resource at https://tedthomas.com & https://www.taxlienlady.com

Personal Story

I first got exposed to tax lien investing when I read The 16% Solution...How To Get High Interest Rates in a Low Interest World With Tax Lien Certificates by Attorney Joel S. Moskowitz. This was over a decade ago, and when I got exposed to it, I was fascinated at the opportunity to not only earn the high interest rates associated with it, but to also potentially gain ownership of a property at pennies on the dollar.

Now, that doesn't happen a lot of the time...general statistics are that about 3% of all tax liens end up with a resulting transfer of ownership to the person who purchased the tax lien. But 97% of the time, either the bank or the homeowner steps up to the plate and satisfies the lien, and you end up earning a cool 16% to 36% on your money, depending on the state and county in question.

Growth Model #4: Real Estate Investing

You can Diversify your portfolio by buying, holding, and selling real estate for non-correlated returns to the stock market, and passive income. With traditional real estate investing, you use your own money to find deals to buy and hold or to flip for an immediate profit.

On the creative side of real estate investing, you can learn to profit from deals without ever having your money in the deal, but instead using other people's money, or simply gain control of a good deal with the right contractual agreements, and then broker that deal out to others, for an easy $5,000 to $10,000 per deal as what's referred to in the industry as a "bird dog."

Potential Cash On Cash Return: 25% to 100% for 3 to 12 months (deal specific)

DIY Resource at https://www.roofstockacademy.com/

Personal Story

My first run at making 7 Figures was largely in part to profits I made from real estate investing in my twenties, a few decades ago. I had a team I worked with that facilitated buying and flipping properties in Atlanta, and, at one point, I had a portfolio of about a dozen properties.

The only time I ever lost my job was when other employees I worked with got jealous, because they heard me wheeling and dealing during my lunch hour break at my office using our company phone. I got written up, and eventually was let go for using company resources for personal benefit, and that led to a discrimination charge for unjust termination, but that's another story for another day.

Experiences like that and others are a subtle reminder of why my time in corporate working for someone else was short lived.

Growth Model #5: Intimate Stock Investing

You can accelerate the growth of your portfolio by building intimacy with a handful of stocks so you know when to buy, hold, and sell them for massive profits.

Forget everything you've heard about owning a diversified portfolio of stocks. Not that the advice is wrong, it's just not the most profitable.

If you want to average returns over the long term that are similar to or worse than the 10% average annual return on the S&P 500 since its inception in the 1920's, then maintain a diversified portfolio.

But, for massive returns, you'll get to know a handful of blue chip stocks intimately, so you can predictably profit from their cyclical moves up and down.

Potential Return: 20% to 100% for 12 months (skill specific)

DIY Resource at https://www.warriortrading.com/trading-courses/

Personal story

Early as a child, I fell in love with the idea of owning a piece of a company, and have invested in this space on and off for most of my career. I started off like most did buying mutual funds, then learned they were not the most optimal choice. As I continued my learning in this space, I discovered this method of intimate stock investing where you can deliver "Alpha," or earn higher returns than the average indices, with a concentrated portfolio rather than with a diversified portfolio.

The key to this is not just to buy and hold like most do, but rather to buy, hold, and sell through their cyclical, repetitive, and sometimes predictable movements up and down.

Growth Model #6: Blue Chip Art Investing

Rather than just inspiring your creativity or bringing a home to life, that Mona Lisa painting, sitting in your living room, can actually help you build a diversified portfolio at minimized risk.

Due to the low correlation to other markets and consistent growth over the last 60 years, many savvy investors are putting 10-20% of their wealth in this asset class.

As a matter of fact, if you wanted to handsomely beat the S&P 500's average annual return for about the past two decades, all you had to do was own a position in blue chip art, that's now a $1.7 Trillion market.

Here's a little known fact. It's worth noting that: ART was the best performing asset class of 2019 & it outperformed the S&P 500 by over 180% between 2000 & 2018.

Potential Return: 8.9% Average Annual ROR

DIY Resource at http://bluechipartco.com/art-investing and https://wcc.art/investment

Personal story

I haven't participated in this space yet, but I am all for having access to opportunities to outperform the market, which is why we've included this asset class as one of our top 9 wealth growth models.

Growth Model #7: Fractional Life Settlements

When a senior no longer wants or needs their permanent life insurance policies, rather than surrender for cash value, they can be sold for as much as 4X the cash value. Investors buy policies in one of three ways.

First, if you have a million or more lying around and can expertly perform due diligence on your own, you can directly purchase a policy.

Second, rather than direct ownership, you can join a pool of investors, and own a portion of the pool through fractional life settlements.

Third, you can purchase shares in a private equity fund that owns hundreds of policies to provide diversification in this asset class.

Notable Investors: Institutional Investors, Hedge Funds, Buffet, & Gates

Potential Return: 12.4% Average Annual ROR (policy specific)

DIY Resource at https://www.themcgriffalliance.com/why-life-settlements-make-sense

Personal Story

These kinds of investments were historically reserved for institutional investors, hedge funds, and the uber wealthy. But, as with all things, over the course of time, opportunities have been created for accredited investors, and some rank and file folks, to access these types of investments through funds, and other fractional ownership opportunities.

Warren Buffet and Bill Gates both speak highly of and have billions invested in this.

Growth Model #8: Foreign Currency Investing

Ever wonder how the major banks make their money? Using your money on deposit to profit from the FOREX market is one way.

It's the largest financial market in the world providing a place for investors to buy, sell, exchange, and speculate on currencies like the dollar, euro, yen and more. Top reasons people like FOREX are:

1. Highly accessible (24/5 & as little as $500 to open an account).
2. More equality (large size, levels playing field, avoids manipulation).
3. Extremely liquid with $6.6 trillion traded daily.
4. Very profitable with potential to 10X investment in a short time.

Notable: Millennials and individuals make up 90% of this trading market yet lose on 90% of their trades. Institutional investors make up 10% of the trading market yet win on 90% of their trades

Potential Return: 5% to 25% Average Monthly ROR (professional traders)

DIY Resource at https://www.fxacademy.com & https://www.forexsignals.com

Personal Story

Probably one of the most fascinating of all of these top 9 wealth accumulation models is the opportunity to invest in the FOREX market. It's an area where myself and clients of mine have benefited greatly.

There are scores of people I know who in less than a year have seen their account values triple and are on pace to fully retire from simply mastering the FOREX market as either an active or a passive investor.

Growth Model #9: Initial Public Offerings (IPOs)

You can accelerate the growth of wealth by not just investing in household name stocks, but by investing in what could potentially become the next breed of household name stocks when you invest in an IPO.

In an IPO, a privately owned company lists its shares on a stock exchange, making them available for purchase by the general public. Often, there's more demand than supply for a new IPO, thus there is seldom a guarantee those interested in an IPO will be able to purchase the shares.

Although shares can be purchased through a brokerage firm, those allotments are often reserved for larger clients. While there's money to be made with an IPO, the real money, however, is made in gaining access to the shares at PRE-IPO prices. That's something very few people have access to.

Notable Investors: Institutional Investors, Hedge Funds, Private Clients

Potential Return: 5% to 100% Initial Annual ROR (IPO specific)

DIY Resource at https://www.sofi.com/invest/ipo-investing

Personal Story

Traditionally, access to IPOs were reserved for large institutional investors. But today, even non-institutional investors are getting access to participate in IPOs.

In chapter 12 on the 5 Ways We Guarantee Our Client's Success, I share some PRE-IPO deals that I'm in, and that our clients have access to as well. PRE IPO's are generally more profitable than IPO's.

When it comes to accelerating the creation of wealth, I started off this second part of the book by highlighting strategies on how to find a high income earning opportunity, how to avoid the "mom and dad plan," how to avoid the perils of the financial services industry, and how to minimize the impact of taxation.

I've concluded this part of the book by discussing my list of the top 9 wealth growth models for you to consider. I've also shared some personal notes and personal stories on each model. More importantly, I've provided some "DIY" resources for those who want to learn more and implement this into your overall wealth growth plan.

Want to discover how I'm helping my clients passively use these top 9 wealth growth models to shrink financial independence timelines from 30 years to as little as 2 years, so you can fulfill your purpose, while enjoying six figures in passive income as you pursue purpose-driven passion projects you love, that can change the world?

Then, I invite you to book a strategy session with myself or a member of my team. I have limited spots available for these calls, so if you'd like to secure a spot on me or a member of my team's calendar, do so here:
http://call.manifestwealthsafely.com

In the next part of this book, I'll show you *"How To Guarantee Your Wealth Success"* by starting off with a discussion in chapter 11 on The 5 Reasons We Fail To Achieve Our Financial Goals. But first, here are a few chapter reflection questions for you.

FOR REFLECTION:

1. What's the most significant personal finance and wealth growth lesson you've learned?
2. How has the lesson you learned from question #1 above changed how you manage your personal finance and wealth accumulation goals?
3. Do you understand how your money is currently invested and the "businesses" of the stocks or other investments you own?
4. What are your thoughts on Warren Buffet's Top 2 Rules Of Investing and how are you incorporating them into your personal finance and wealth accumulation plans?
5. Given what you now know about my list of Top 9 wealth accumulation models, which one are you most interested in learning more about and incorporating into your wealth accumulation plan?

PART 3

How To **Guarantee Your Wealth Success**

CHAPTER 11

5 Reasons We Fail To Achieve Our Financial Goals

"That which we manifest is before us; we are the creators of our own destiny. Be it through intention or ignorance, our successes, and our failures have been brought on by none other than ourselves."

~ Garth Stein ~

In part 1 of this book you learned about Why Purpose Is Key To Being Wealthy. In part 2, I shared How To Accelerate The Creation Of Wealth.

In this third part of the book, you'll discover How To Guarantee Your Wealth Success.

We'll start off our journey on how to guarantee your wealth success by first identifying the 5 reasons we fail to achieve our financial goals. After all, as creative beings, we are perpetually creating the realities we face daily.

Reason #1: We Don't Understand The Wealth Creation Gap

Most of us spend our lives paying compound interest instead of earning it. And the vast majority of us sit on the wrong side of the wealth creation versus working population fence. Let me try to explain this with a deeper dive into the picture from everyone's RICH DAD, Robert Kiyosaki.

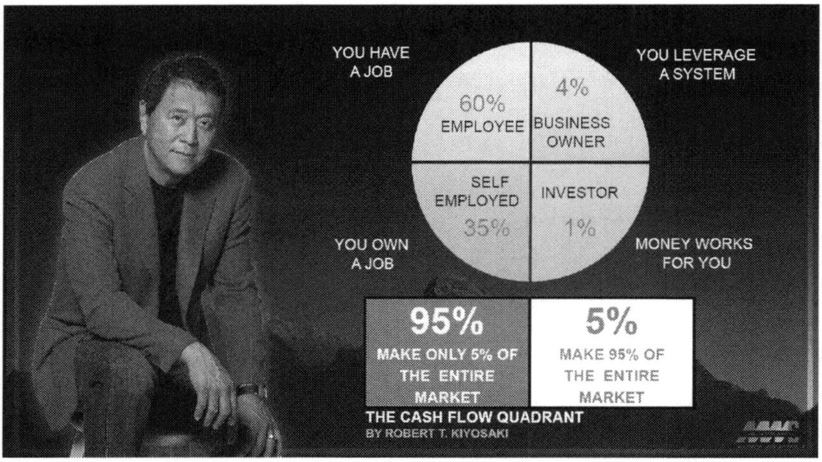

All we have to do is look at Robert Kiyosaki's CashFlow Quadrant to recognize the amazing gap between the working population versus where all the wealth actually is. And, what we see on one side of the quadrant, is that 95% of our working population is made up of employees, and self-employed people like lawyers, consultants, coaches, and even doctors. Yet, they only control 5% of the total wealth.

But, over on the other side of the quadrant, we see that while Business Owners, and Investors, make up just 5% of our working population, they are the ones who control 95% of the total wealth. So, rather than the "ES" side of the Quadrant, where you want to be is in the "BI" side of the Quadrant. It's important to recognize this very important dynamic about wealth creation.

Reason #2: We Don't Understand The Importance Of The 7 Realms Of Wealth

One of the greatest tragedies I've experienced, and seen in the life of others, is to wish upon a thing, like financial wealth, get it, then have it leave you emptier than before you had it. When it comes to wealth, me must understand that there are 7 realms of wealth namely:

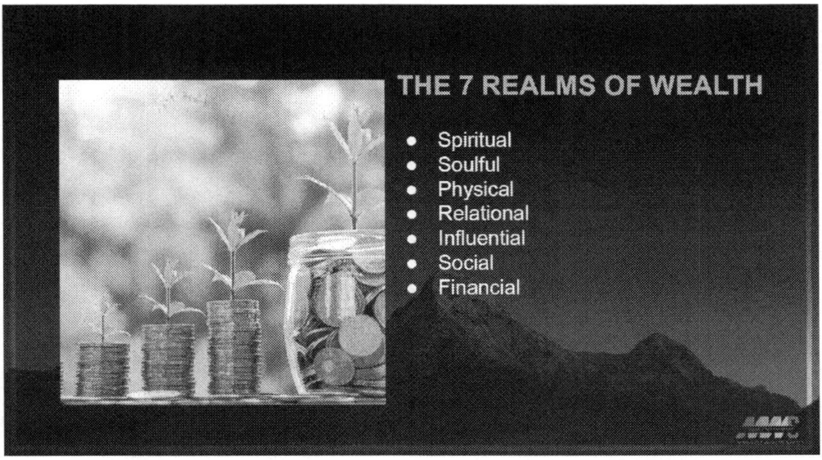

- **Spiritual:** which deals with how wealthy your relationship is with the creator of the universe.
- **Soulful:** looks at how wealthy your mind, will, and emotions are based on what you're feeding it.
- **Physical:** there is no real wealth to be enjoyed without one's physical health.
- **Relational:** how wealthy are the relationships you have with those you love.
- **Influential:** how wealthy are you in your ability to influence others decisions.
- **Social:** how wealthy are you in making your community better. Do you sit on company boards as an example, and are you actively improving your community?
- **Financial:** this one obviously speaks for itself.

It's been my experience, and the experience of others, that if all you do in this life is acquire financial wealth, without these other 6 realms of wealth, you will self-sabotage, lose all the financial wealth you acquired, and live an empty life.

Take it from a guy who's made and lost 7-Figures of wealth twice when I tell you that you can't be truly wealthy, without being wealthy in all 7 realms of wealth.

Reason #3: We're Working Hard To Accumulate Wealth Instead Of Working Smarter

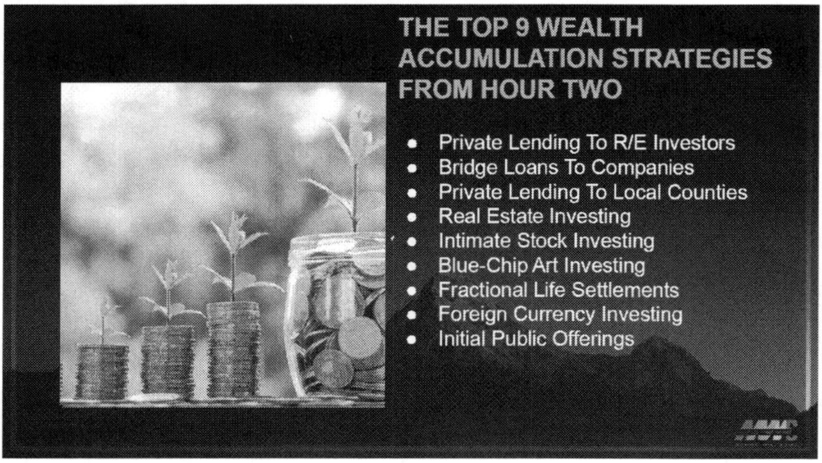

One of the greatest fallacies to wealth success is the idea of working hard. The most successful people I know have mastered the art of automating, delegating and eliminating. As I shared these Top 9 wealth accumulation strategies from chapter 10 in part 2 of this book, there are likely two categories of people that emerged as I discussed those strategies.

Category #1 is someone who believes in working harder, who might have said, I need to learn more about these 9 strategies, so I can implement them in my personal wealth growth plan. If that's you, the DIY Resources in that chapter will undoubtedly serve you well.

However, Category #2 is someone who believes in working smarter, who might have said, I'd much rather eliminate the hassle of having to learn the intricacies of how to do this on my own, and instead automate, by delegating this to someone else, and just passively benefit from the opportunity that each one of these provides to grow my wealth.

If you're of the Category #2 types, then you are in luck. In our Manifest Wealth Safely Program, what we do is provide the opportunity for you to passively benefit from these Top 9 and other wealth accumulation strategies, while affording you the opportunity to geek out and learn more about each of these on your own time, if you so choose to do so.

I'm all for working smarter, not harder, when it comes to achieving my wealth accumulation goals. I don't want to, nor do I need to be, an expert, or even an active participant in any of these opportunities...especially if I can passviley profit from all of them without lifting a finger. If you want to do the same, just book a call with me here:

http://call.manifestwealthsafely.com

Reason #4: We're Still Using 20th Century Models In A 21st Century Investing Economy

Let me introduce you to what should potentially be a life-changing moment for each of you reading this book, as you discover the future of building wealth through the power of artificial intelligence technology, and investing in FOREX, the largest financial market on the planet.

If you've ever flown into London, England, as an example, (a place where we had a home growing up as a kid) and had to exchange US Dollars for British Pounds while in the country, you know you make that exchange at specific rates. And, when you fly back into the USA, and exchange any leftover pounds for dollars, that exchange could be at a totally different rate.

These rates change all the time, but the ability to move from one currency to another in order to transact business is what makes up the FOREX market.

The stock market, which is where most people have their money invested, trades about $200 billion dollars per day. In comparison, the FOREX market trades $6.6 Trillion dollars a day. It is the largest financial market that exists and trades 24 hours a day, 5 days a week, on any device, and it focuses on CASH or FIAT currency.

The Crypto Market, on the other hand, is an unregulated market which trades 24 hours a day, 7 days a week. If you've ever heard about Bitcoin as an example, that's one form of a digital currency traded in this market. This market is anticipated to hit 1 trillion dollars, so it's growing very rapidly.

And, whether we like it or not, whether we're prepared for it or not, all indications point to digital currency being the norm through which payments will be made in our not too distant future. So, it's likely not going to be a bad idea to become more familiar with this space.

How AI Is Changing Everything

All of the recent data out there shows that AI will replace 50% of jobs in the next decade. Just a few of the industries that AI is already impacting include the automotive industry with the advent of self driving cars. It's impacting consumer buying decisions with Alexa, Siri and the like. The Logistics, Recruiting, Insurance and Law Industries are all evolving with AI. And, in the FINTECH space, JP Morgan, UBS and other big banks use AI to reduce risk, increase accuracy, and enhance trading results in the FOREX markets.

AI's Impact In The Wealth Management Space

To get a sense of the kind of impact AI is having in this space, here's what you find from some recent articles:

- » July 31, 2021 fxxsi.com article notes that while retail traders (you and I) lose 90% of the time in FOREX, the smart money traders (banks and financial institutions) win 90% of the time.
- » July 6, 2017 Financial Times ft.com article notes that robots enter investment banks trading floors with UBS among the banks looking to AI to boost traders performance.
- » Aug 1, 2017 Financeefeeds.com article notes JPMorgan, the world's largest investment bank by revenue, says it's the first large Tier 1 financial institution to use AI with trade execution and said it would take rivals 18 to 24 months and an investment of multiple millions to come up with similar technology.
- » April 7, 2020 Aiauthority.com article notes that AI is in fact the future of FOREX Trading.

Now, with that as a backdrop, here's a quote from yours truly that's worth paying attention to, if you're seriously interested in accelerating the realization of your wealth accumulation goals.

"To guarantee your success in Living Your Life on FIRE...Financially Independent And Retired Early, you don't always have to innovate. Sometimes you can just follow the smart money and replicate what's working as in the case of FOREX AI Investing"

- ***Ike Ikokwu***

And that's exactly what we've done and generated exceptional results.

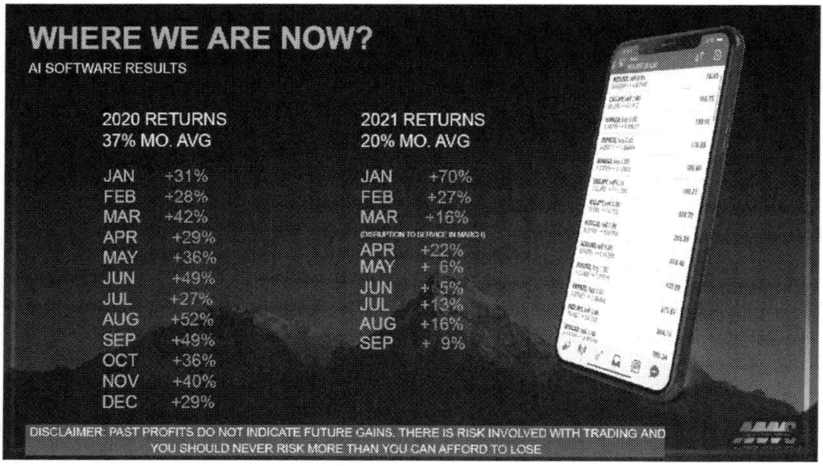

Now, I need to make my attorneys happy and share this disclosure: "Past Profits Do Not Indicate Future Gains. There Is Risk Involved With Trading The FOREX Markets And You Should Never Risk More Than You Can Afford To Lose."

With that said, the chart above are monthly returns from an AI software that myself, my clients, and thousands of other wealth creators have benefited from.

In 2020, the monthly average return was 37% and honestly, in 2021, we've not done as well as we did in 2020.

With September 2021 year to date cumulative returns of 184% in just 9 months, we're sitting at a little over 20% in monthly average returns for 2021.

What I've found is Success in life is often defined not so much by what you know, but rather who you know, and maybe more importantly, who knows you. So, it pays to be in the right "Network."

And, while I just shared results from the AI software itself, here are results from one of my individual accounts:

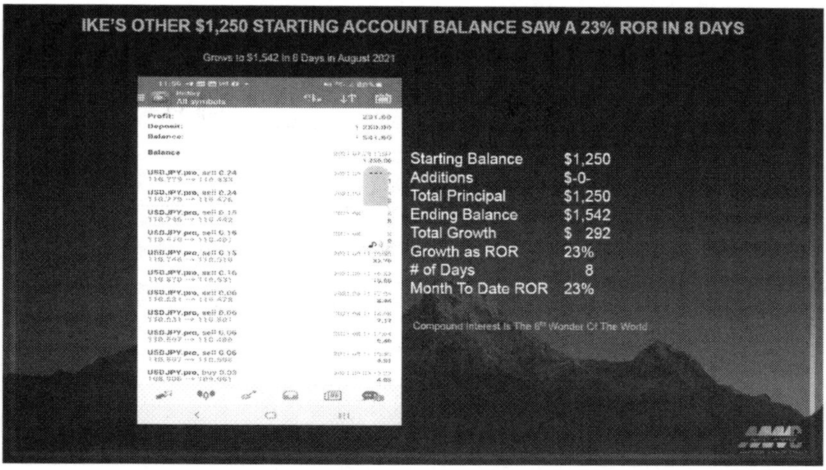

The above screenshot shows the kind of success I'm having with utilizing artificial intelligence in the FOREX market.

This one account generated a 23% return within just the first 8 trading days of August 2021 in the FOREX market.

With those kinds of profits, is it any wonder why Albert Einstein is quoted as saying compound interest is the 8th wonder of the world?

PRE-IPO INVESTING

"To guarantee your success in Living Your Life on FIRE...Financially Independent And Retired Early, you don't always have to innovate. Sometimes you can just follow the smart money and replicate what's working as in the case of PRE IPO Investing"

- ***Ike Ikokwu***

I'm about to share with you PRE-IPO Investing, another 21st Century Investing Model that I'm using to help my clients and I to guarantee their wealth success.

Why Pre-IPOs

In 2008, Congress passed legislation allowing ground floor investing to all Americans, but it still has been kept secretive to the masses up to this point. Ridiculously large gains that used to be only for the rich and powerful can now be possible for everyone.

A pre-IPO investment occurs when the fund managers connect selling insiders to accredited investors of the hottest upcoming IPOs before they hit the market. Through our strategic partnerships, we connect private investors to the best funds to obtain those shares.

By choosing the strongest disruptors in their industries, your opportunity moves beyond buying, to cherry-picking the best opportunities in the world for your portfolio, maximizing your profits for your portfolio.

Past Performance From PRE-IPO Investing With Our Strategic Partner

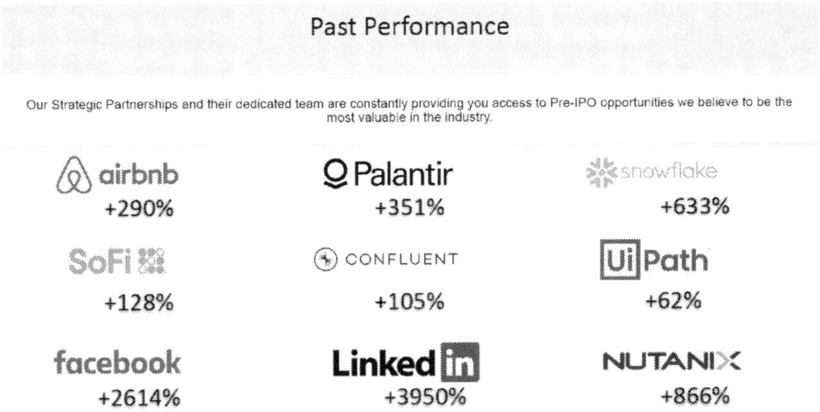

I'm sure you recognize several of the names of the PRE-IPO companies our strategic partner has provided access to over the years.

And while I just shared results from PRE-IPO Investing with strategic partners we work with, here is some information on 1 of 3 PRE-IPO positions we are sitting on as of October, 2021:

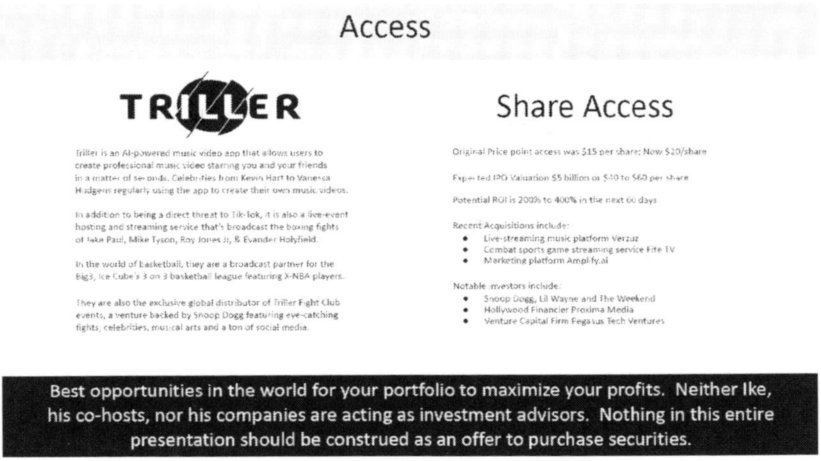

The above screenshot tells you a bit about Triller's business model, what our share access price point has been, as well as who some notable investors in the company are.

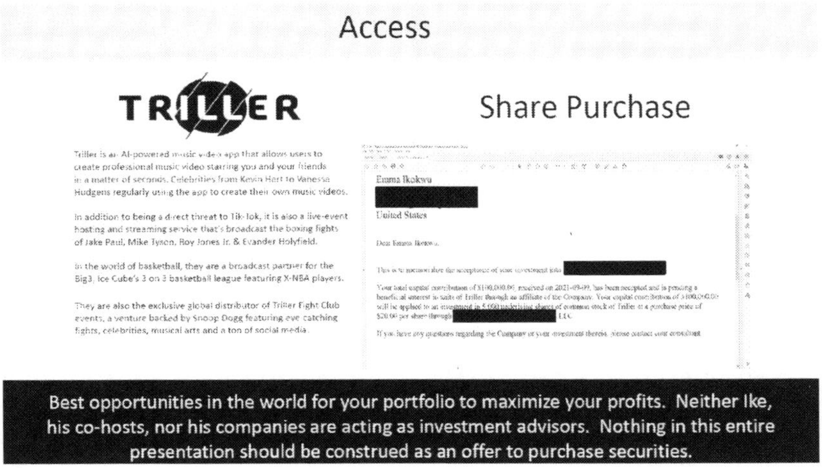

The above screenshot shows you the 5,000 share position we've taken in Triller at $20 per share. Our expectation is to see a 200% to 400% return on investment over the next 60 to 90 days on this position when it hits the market.

PRODUCTIVE DEBT

"All debt isn't bad. There's unproductive debt, which is the silent killer to wealth accumulation. Then, there's productive debt, which can be a catalyst to wealth accumulation. One example of productive debt is bridge lending to corporations"

- ***Ike Ikokwu***

I'm about to share with you Bridge Loans To Companies, another 21st Century Investing Model that I'm using to help my clients and I to guarantee their wealth success.

Bridge Loans To Companies As An Example of Productive Debt

I've already described in chapter 10 how these types of loans work. What I want to do is show you an example of one of the three tranches of this that I participated in during 2021 to earn 20% on my money over a 95 day term.

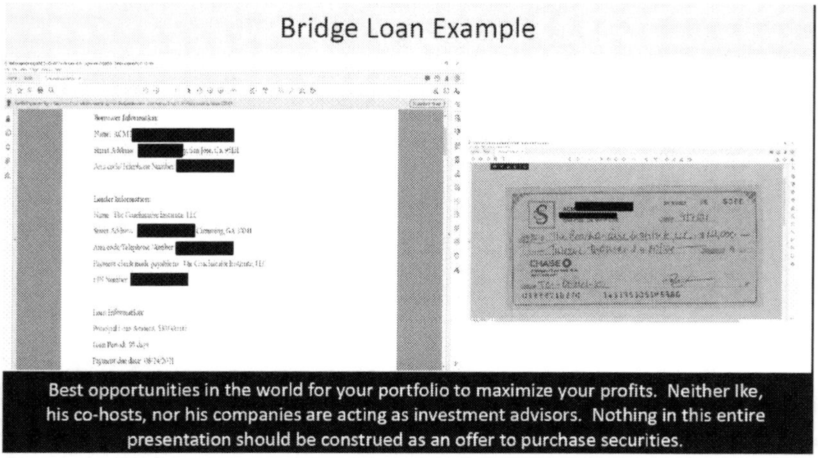

As you can see in the screenshot above, one of my companies placed $10,000 on a 95 day term bridge loan to a company due 8/24/21. And, you can see the check that was dated 9/7/21 for $12,000 returning our original principal of $10,000 plus a $2,000 (20%) return on investment.

Reason #5: Most Traverse Life Without A Clue About What Our Owner's Manual Says

One of the greatest travesties I saw in the financial services industry was people who worked for 30 years in a job they hated, but with an eye on the clock to their 30 year retirement date, when they'd start "living."

Who thinks part of our owner's manual says we are to hate and waste 30 years of our life? I don't think that's part of our original design. Let me explain.

> "It's more tragic to be alive and not know why,
> than to be dead and not know life"
>
> \- *Dr. Myles Munroe*

If you've read this far into the book, you know the kind of influence Dr. Munroe has had on my life. But how do we solve this dilemma Dr. Munroe refers to? How do we discover our purpose? How do we find out what our owner's manual says?

Finding Your WHY

Well, if you've read part 1 of this book, you know I went over a 5 step process to help you identify your life and your business purpose. Then, I even talked about our strategic partnership with the WHY Institute, to help you discover your WHY and your WHY Operating System. All of this is so you can take Simon Sinek's EPIC work and make it practical. So, this way, you not only know your WHY, but you also know your HOW, and your WHAT.

Now, When it comes to my WHY, my PURPOSE, it's really multi-faceted. Through a series of divine events, one thing the Lord laid on my heart in 2021 was to launch the Righteous Billionaire Movement.
And, that Movement, helps to further my various causes. Some of which include:

» Helping end hopelessness;
» Fighting against human trafficking; and
» Awakening the sleeping giant, that is also known as "The Church"

And, in the process, to also sound a clarion call for how important it is that as a nation, we have righteous leaders at the helm of each of the 7 major spheres of our culture. Leaders who not only will lead righteously, but who also have the financial capital to make the necessary changes in our society.

Wondering what the 7 spheres of culture are that I speak of? They include the:

» Media - for those that aren't aware, the media is owned by 6 major corporations AT&T, CBS, Comcast, Disney, Newscorp and Viacom. Now, one has to ask: does the value of these 6 companies align with yours?
» Government - which it doesn't matter if you're Democrat or Republican, I think we'd agree that both parties could use a little reform, right?
» Education - most would agree our education system is broken. One of my coaches, David Bayer, actually has a plan to reform the education system, when he runs for President in 2032.
» Economy - while there's a board of governors that oversee the Federal Reserve, it is not under control of any branch of the federal gov-

ernment.

» Family - the fact that it is being redefined daily is heartbreaking to me.
» Religion - one has to ask what kind of influence the church is having in this sphere?
» Arts & Entertainment - Artists like Lil Nas X, with his devil inspired shoes, and others in this space, that continue to push the boundaries of what's tasteful and acceptable in our culture. At what point does one take a stance on good clean entertainment?

What Are The Necessary Changes In Our Society That I Desire To See?

Those changes could include buying up the major media empires that exist today, in order to restore a sense of decency and morality with the entertainment choices that are available. Or, it might include starting media empires that drown out the noise from the existing ones.

Another sphere of culture that's ripe for change is Politics. And, for those who want to go into politics, we're partnering with an organization that will provide access to the training, coaching and resources necessary to raise up righteous politicians, who'll know how to effectively prepare for, run, and win political offices at the city, state and national levels, in order to shift the appalling nature of leadership we find presently in politics.

Listen, I can't overstate the importance of finding your WHY or allowing it to find you. Because when you do, it adds a certain ZEST and FIRE to your life.

That's what it's done for me and so I'm committed to helping others do the same, while at the same time becoming financially independent. I've said this before and I'll say it again, everything you've ever hoped and dreamed of, is on the other side of finding your purpose, and discovering your why.

That's why the entire first part of this book was dedicated to helping you recognize why purpose is the key to being wealthy.

In this chapter, I've shown you the 5 reasons we fail to achieve our financial goals, and given you 3 examples of how we deploy passive income, and wealth creation strategies, to take advantage of 3 of the top 9 wealth growth models we introduced you to in chapter 10.

Want to discover how I'm helping my clients avoid the 5 reasons most fail to achieve their financial goals and shrink financial independence timelines from 30 years to as little as 2 years, so you can fulfill your purpose, while enjoying six figures in passive income, as you pursue purpose-driven passion projects you love, that can change the world?

Then, I invite you to book a strategy session with myself, or a member of my team. I have limited spots available for these calls, so if you'd like to secure a spot on me or a member of my team's calendar, do so here:
http://call.manifestwealthsafely.com

In the next chapter, I'll show you the 5 Ways We Guarantee Our Clients Success as the second step to guarantee your wealth success. But first, here are a few chapter reflection questions for you.

FOR REFLECTION:

1. What can you do to move to the "Business Owner/Investor" side of the CashFlow Quadrant?
2. What steps are you taking to maximize the 7 realms of wealth?
3. How can you transition from working hard to working smarter to accumulate wealth?
4. What are you doing to ensure you're not stuck using 20th century models in a 21st century investing economy?
5. What steps have you taken to ensure you know what your owner's manual says?

CHAPTER 12

5 Ways We Guarantee Our Client's Success

"Whether you think you can, or you think you can't - you're right."

~ Henry Ford ~

In the last chapter, we started off our journey in this third part of the book on how to guarantee your wealth success, by helping you identify the 5 reasons we fail to achieve our financial goals.

We'll continue that journey in this chapter by showing you 5 ways we guarantee our client's success.

I often like to ask my business owner clients what business they are in? When I do, they go into elaborate details about the products and services they offer to their customers, and clients, and how those products, and services, help their customers and clients.

Once they are done with their elaborate discussions, I then ask them another question. I ask them if they want to know what business they are really in. After a bit of a puzzled look, they eventually go, "sure, tell me."

It's then I explain to them that the business they are really in is the "Belief Changing" business. Regardless of what product or service they sell, every customer or client has a belief that's diametrically opposed to what you think your product, service, or value proposition can do for them. Until you change their belief system, you don't have a new customer or client.

Over the course of this book I've been very intentional about causing a paradigm shift to occur in what you think is possible for you to be, do, and have, as it relates to experiencing an abundance of wealth in all seven of its realms.

From the various chapters in part 1 of this book on Why Purpose is Key To Being Wealthy, to the chapters in part 2 on How To Accelerate The Creation Of Wealth, to the chapters in part 3 on How To Guarantee Your Wealth Success, I've been very intentional about shifting your belief system.

As a former licensed investment advisor, I know that when you talk about success with your money or wealth, and you start using the word "guarantee," it throws up all kinds of alarms. So, I want to be very clear on my use of the word 'guarantee,' as it relates to the contents of this book, and what I can do for you.

I can't guarantee the rates of return you'll earn on any wealth accumulation opportunities we might introduce to you. I can't guarantee that you'll be a millionaire, or a billionaire, by following the advice in this book, or any recommendations I make, should you become a client. I can't even guarantee you'll earn the same kinds of returns I've earned on any of the top 9 wealth growth models I and my clients use, as outlined in chapter 10 of this book.

But, here is what I can guarantee. I can guarantee to provide you with the education, coaching, mentorship, customer service, and access to wealth growth opportunities that can make the lofty goals espoused in this book a reality for you.

To be even more specific, here is our Quintuple or 5-Part Service Guarantee:

1. **Avoid The Wealth Creation Gap Mistake Guarantee**: We put you on the right side of Robert Kiyosaki's CashFlow Quadrant by offering you opportunities to be an investor, and if you choose, to also be a business owner.

2. **Seven Realms Of Wealth Guarantee**: We provide coaching and mentoring to raise the next generation of leaders that have the

leadership and financial capital to implement righteous changes in our society.

3. **Outsourced Passive Wealth Creation Guarantee**: Rather than having to actively learn and benefit from the top 9 wealth accumulation strategies on your own, within our Manifest Wealth Safely Program, we provide ways for you to benefit from them, and other Family Office type opportunities, without the $100,000, or $1 million minimums, normally required to participate in them.

4. **21st Century Wealth Accumulation Model Guarantee**: We put you on the cutting edge of wealth accumulation, not by innovating the brightest strategies, but by simply replicating what the smart money (Top Tier Banks and Financial Institutions) is doing, using Artificial Intelligence (AI) Technology as an example, to accelerate the growth of wealth.

5. **Unlock Your Purpose Guarantee**: In partnership with the WHY Institute, and through our coaching and mentoring, we will help ensure that you identify, clarify, and magnify your purpose, as you use the leadership and financial capital attained in our program, to pursue purpose-driven passion projects you love, and that have the capacity to change the world.

In addition to our Quintuple Service Guarantee, we also have our Triple Program Guarantee:

1. **Viable Program Guarantee:** If you are accepted into our Manifest Wealth Safely Program (note that there is no fee to apply to see if you qualify), after your initial down payment is made to be a part of the Program, all future payments are deferred. You only share the new wealth or passive income earned. There are no set payments to be in the Manifest Wealth Safely Program to access the coaching, mentoring, training, mastermind, and opportunities you are exposed to help you shrink your financial

independence timeline down from 30 years to as little as 2 to 5 years.

2. **Triple Support Guarantee**: Throughout this wealth creation journey, you get full support from three teams. Those teams are (a) Ike and the Manifest Wealth Safely Team; (b) Expert 7-Figure Traders & Wealth Creators From The Opportunities You Are Exposed To; and (c) Other Subject Matter Experts.

3. **Million Dollar Wealth Creation Guarantee:** We work with you until you've created one million dollars in new wealth, and are enjoying $100,000 in annual passive income.

And last, but certainly not least, is our Overall Program Guarantee:

Overall Program Guarantee: While I can't guarantee the actual rates of returns you'll earn in the program, or that I'll make you a millionaire, or billionaire, I can guarantee to provide you with education, coaching, mentorship, customer service, and access to wealth growth opportunities that can make the lofty goals espoused in this book a reality for you in 2 to 5 years, depending on the amount of capital you deploy to opportunities you get exposed to, and your actual results. Give us 2 to 5 years, and we'll help you create at least $1,000,000 in new wealth, and $100,000 in annual passive income. Ike created this same result for himself when he went from bankrupt in 2003, to financially independent in 2008. This was Ike's personal experience, but there's no guarantee that you will have the same exact experience.

In this chapter, I've shown you the 5 ways we guarantee our client's success, as well as shown you the other guarantees that are incorporated in the agreements with clients that we accept into our Manifest Wealth Safely Program.

Want to discover how these guarantees help my clients avoid the 5 reasons most fail to achieve their financial goals, and shrink financial independence timelines from 30 years to as little as 2 years, so you can fulfill your purpose, while enjoying six figures in passive income, as you pursue purpose-driven passion projects you love, that can change the world?

Then, I invite you to book a strategy session with myself or a member of my team. I have limited spots available for these calls, so if you'd like to secure a spot on me or a member of my team's calendar, do so here:

http://call.manifestwealthsafely.com

In the next chapter, I'll show you what the Manifest Wealth Safely Method, as outlined in this book, can do for you as the third step to guarantee your wealth success. But first, here are a few chapter reflection questions for you.

FOR REFLECTION:

1. What paradigm shifts have occurred for you in the chapters you've read thus far?
2. How is your purpose inextricably connected to your wealth accumulation goals?
3. Would you rather be a business owner, an investor, or both?
4. What's the reason for your answer to question #3 above?
5. How confident are you that you can execute the ideas in this book on your own?

CHAPTER 13

What The Manifest Wealth Safely Method Can Do For You

"Our only limitations are those we set up in our own minds. Whatever the mind can conceive and believe, it can achieve."

~ Napoleon Hill~

In the last chapter, we continued our journey in this third part of the book on how to guarantee your wealth success by sharing 5 ways we guarantee our client's success.

We'll conclude that journey in this chapter by showing you what the Manifest Wealth Safely Method can do for you.

In the prior chapter, I talked about how business owners need to recognize that the real business they are in is the "Belief Changing" business. I've started this chapter with a quote from one of my favorite authors, Napoleon Hill, on the importance of expanding the realms of what's possible for us by tapping into the power of our belief system.

I began this book, in the introduction, by noting that as complex a subject as the subject of this book might sound, the entirety of this book can be summed up in the following three steps for each group of those who have $100,000 in liquid net worth, and for those who don't

Those three steps for those who don't have $100,000 in liquid net worth are:

Step #1:
Find a High-Income Earning Opportunity: Simply put, the quickest way to 10X your income is as an entrepreneur. This book didl highlight one of the best opportunities to become an entrepreneur, and build a Seven-Figure business in 2 years or less, even if you know nothing about sales, marketing, or technology.

Step #2:
Find a High-Growth Wealth Building Opportunity: Once you understand why Albert Einstein labelled compound interest the eight wonder of the world, you'll want to have a love affair with it, to increase the velocity of wealth creation.

Step #3:
Find a Passive Income Creation Opportunity: If compound interest is the eight wonder of the world, I believe passive income is the 9th wonder of the world. Once you understand this, you'll appreciate why Warren Buffet says "if you don't find a way to make money while you sleep, you will work until you die."

Those three steps for those who already have $100,000 in liquid net worth are:

Step #1:
Discover Your Purpose: I believe that it's more tragic to have wealth and not know why, than to have death and not know life. If you already have $100,000 in liquid net worth, you've at least taken the first step to creating wealth. What you now want to do is accelerate the creation of wealth, but not before you discover what you'll do with that wealth. If we were all created on purpose and for purpose, then it's our responsibility to figure out what that purpose is, because, as I've said before, all that we desire in life and in business, as well as the mark and impact we are to have on earth, all of that sits on the other side of our purpose.

Step #2:

Find a High-Growth Wealth Building Opportunity: Once you understand why Albert Einstein labelled compound interest the eight wonder of the world, you'll want to have a love affair with it, to increase the velocity of wealth creation.

Step #3:
Find a Passive Income Creation Opportunity: If compound interest is the eight wonder of the world, I believe passive income is the 9th wonder of the world. Once you understand this, you'll appreciate why Warren Buffet says "if you don't find a way to make money while you sleep, you will work until you die."

I illustrated what the outcome would be for my client, Jill, who fits the category of those who already have $100,000 in liquid net worth. Her case study is worth representing here again.

Jill's Case Study On Minimizing The Impact Of Taxation

One of the clients I'm working with presently is the perfect example of a Jill "Do What Everybody Else Does." We'll call her Jill for the purposes of our discussion. Jill is 59 years old and works in Management for a company and makes right at about $100,000 a year.

Her husband, we'll call him Jack, just went on disability 3 years ago but only got "qualified" a year or so ago to draw a small disability income check.

Jill's story is pretty typical to what I see with many clients I work with.

She started saving when she was 18 years old and built up a nice nest egg in her employer sponsored 401K saving account. Then, the 2008 market crash hit and she lost 60% of her life savings just like that.

As if that wasn't bad enough, she also lost her job. Fortunately for her, she found a loophole that allowed her to borrow funds from her account and access that remaining 40% to help her navigate those difficult times.

She borrowed the remaining money in her retirement plan with the intention of paying it back. Well, you know what they say about the best of intentions, right? She never followed through on that.

Thankfully, over the years and with a little cooperation from the stock market, she's built her 401K account at her new employer back up to about a $125,000 balance.

When she first started working with me, she felt like she was woefully behind the "8-Ball," in preparing for a secure financial future, and thought she might have to work the rest of her life to be secure, as well as to provide the kind of financial assistance her grandkids would need, when they eventually, and prematurely lose their mom due to a debilitating health issue.

Her situation seemed hopeless, or so she thought. That was, until I revealed the Manifest Wealth + 6 Figure Roadmap I'd put together for her.

Using a combination of the strategies to enjoy tax-free income in chapter 9, and coupling that with what you learned in chapter 10 on the top 9 wealth growth models, chapter 11 on the 5 reasons we fail to achieve our financial goals, and chapter 12 on the 5 ways we guarantee our client's success, Jill and her family will have a very bright financial future in as little as 5 years.

Specifically, the roadmap we've put together will take her $125,000 fully taxable 401K plan balance and turn it into a tax-free wealth haven that in 5 years, will be worth about $5.3 million.

At that point, she can comfortably take $500,000 a year in tax-free income, and still see her account balance continue to grow.

This plan ensures she not only retires ahead of plan at age 64, but that she enjoys six-figures in tax-free income, while she pursues her purpose-driven passion projects and creates the kind of financial legacy she wants to create for her children and grandchildren.

Is There Any Hope For Those Who Don't Have $100,000 In Liquid Net Worth?

Calculation Projection

Future investment value
$1,327,217.44

Total interest earned
$1,307,217.44

Initial balance
$20,000.00

Effective Annual Rate (APY)
131.41%

Summary

Initial deposit: $20,000.00
Interest rate: 7% monthly
Time: 5 years
Compounding: daily (360/year)

Projection breakdown

monthly yearly

Year	Interest	Total Interest	Balance
0	--	--	$20,000.00
1	$26,282.03	$26,282.03	$46,282.03
2	$60,819.29	$87,101.32	$107,101.32
3	$140,742.01	$227,843.34	$247,843.34
4	$325,691.32	$553,534.65	$573,534.65
5	$753,682.79	$1,307,217.44	$1,327,217.44

For those, who don't have $100,000 in liquid net worth like my client Jill, you might have been wondering if there was any hope for a brighter financial future for you?

You might have been wondering if you could also use the Manifest Wealth Safely Method to create a million in new wealth and six figures in passive income in 5 years or less, so you too can pursue purpose-driven passion projects you love that can change the world?

The answer is a resounding yes! As you can see by the chart in the prior page, if all you had was $20,000 of initial capital, and you averaged a 7% monthly return by utilizing one of the top 9 wealth growth models I introduced you to in chapter 10, you can see that in just 5 short years, you'd have $1,307,214, which would easily create six figures in passive income for you, each and every year thereafter.

So, either way you slice it, whether you're starting out the financial gate with $100,000 or more in liquid net worth, or you have less than that, I think you can see that our stated objective of helping you create $1,000,000 in new wealth, and $100,000 in passive income, is very realistic within our Manifest Wealth Safely Program.

Speaking of my Manifest Wealth Safely Program, these are the 5 stages to the program:

Stage 01:

Build Your Wealth Education Foundation

Through the combination of an online learning center/curriculum, group coaching, personal coaching, and mentoring, you'll overcome the biggest problems in financial planning while unlocking wealth building formulas and principles to map out your Roadmap to Manifest Wealth Safely and Create Six Figure Monthly or Annual Passive Income Streams.

Stage 1 Finish Line: *Your new Manifest Wealth + Six Figure Roadmap is designed.*

Stage 1 Prize: *You are confident that you will succeed in manifesting wealth and creating six figures of passive income.*

Stage 02:

Build Your Debt Free Foundation

Through the combination of an online learning center/curriculum, group coaching, personal coaching, and mentoring, you'll discover the true definition of being debt free and you'll extricate yourself from the risks of being ignorant of it.

Stage 2 Finish Line: *You understand the real threat that having or not having debt poses to long term security.*

Stage 2 Prize: *You are satisfied with your plan to be debt free.*

Stage 03:

Launch Your Wealth Accumulation Strategies.

Through the combination of an online learning center/curriculum, group coaching, personal coaching, and mentoring, you identify strategies you want to utilize to earn average real returns from 1% to as much as 25% per month, while converting risky assets into risk-free assets.

Stage 3 Finish Line: *You've identified which strategies to accelerate the growth of your money to manifest wealth safely.*

Stage 3 Prize: *You have accounts growing at a monthly compounded rate of return that some only wish they could earn per annum. You're invited to the Manifest Wealth Safely Mastermind once you have at least $250,000 in newly accumulated wealth from your strategies.*

Stage 04:

Design Your Tax-Free Distribution Strategies.

Through the combination of an online learning center/curriculum, group coaching, personal coaching and mentoring, you initiate a plan to transfer wealth you are accumulating in a taxable environment to an entirely tax-free environment to avoid eroding wealth from high taxation.

Stage 4 Finish Line: *You have a plan to disinherit the IRS from the income stream you receive while alive and the asset you transfer to your heirs upon death.*

Stage 4 Prize: *You know how much in tax-free income you can receive over your lifetime and how much of a tax-free asset you can pass on at death.*

Stage 05:

Monitor and Optimize

At this stage you've added at least one million dollars in new wealth and one hundred thousand dollars in passive income.

You now further identify, clarify, and magnify new purpose-driven passion projects while monitoring and optimizing your plan.

Stage 5 Finish Line: *You will have fully executed your Manifest Wealth + Six Figure Roadmap.*

Stage 5 Prize: *You have at least $1,000,000 in growing wealth, $100,000 in passive income, and you're purposefully pursuing passion projects that you absolutely adore.*

Here's What The Manifest Wealth Safely Method Is Doing For Others:

Dave Sheets

Entrepreneur, President of Outlaw Sales Group, Colorado Springs, Colorado

"I was a financial advisor with Merrill Lynch for, you know, a year and a half. And so, I got, to know, fairly deep into a lot of the instruments that are out there. And I've never seen anything like this. And, you know, five percent doesn't compare to twenty five percent. But, when you take five percent over a year and multiply that out, I mean, you're looking at 60 percent growth, which is incredible"

Gabe Hoover

Teacher, Coach, Entrepreneur, Founder & CEO of YouByDesign, Dublin, Ohio

"But over the last 10 days in the program you set me up in lke, I've made 6% in 10 days. And after getting the account all set up and everything, to be hands off and not have to be a daily trader and just know that the system is working for me, that was, that was both eye opening and encouraging"

Judy Whalen

Entrepreneur, Founder, & The CEO of Whalen & Associates, and The Center for Strategic Change, Brooklyn, Wisconsin

"So now I'm in this program, I have to tell you, it's a hoot! It's actually, it's fun! So, in less than 14 days, I'm up 5.6%. I haven't earned 5% at a bank in years."

Kevin Hailstock

Entrepreneur, Founder and CEO of Web Emerse, LLC, Washington DC

"So, totaling up, a little over five percent for my close to 12 days in the system."

Lois Koffi

Top 20 Podcast Host, Professional Speaker, Sales Trainer & Coach, Entrepreneur, Founder, & The CEO of Lois Koffi Enterprises, Vista, California

"Perhaps you'd share a little bit about some of the 'inside scoop' as to what you've seen so far? Oh my gosh, well last month it was 16 plus percent. This month it's been 6.5% percent and growing. You know, I'm all about data and hard numbers and you've been very transparent about showing how this is possible. And yes, there's no guarantees, I get all that. But you have a track record, you have other clients who have a track record"

When it comes to guaranteeing your wealth success, I started off this third part of the book by introducing you to the 5 reasons we fail to achieve our financial goals, and the 5 ways we guarantee our client's success.

I've concluded this part of the book by showing you what the Manifest Wealth Safely Method can do for you, whether you have $100,000 in liquid net worth, or whether you have significantly less than that.

Want to discover how I'm helping my clients incorporate everything I've shared in this book, passively, to shrink financial independence timelines from 30 years to as little as 2 years, so you can fulfill your purpose, while enjoying six figures in passive income, as you pursue purpose-driven passion projects you love, that can change the world?

Then, I invite you to book a strategy session with myself or a member of my team. I have limited spots available for these calls, so if you'd like to secure a spot on me or a member of my team's calendar, do so here:

http://call.manifestwealthsafely.com

In the next part of this book, I'll bring this book to a conclusion by showing you how to get started on your wealth building adventure, with discussions on What To Do Next, How To Get More Help and giving you a quick biography on yours truly. But first, here are a few chapter reflection questions for you.

FOR REFLECTION:

1. What self-limiting beliefs could preclude you from realizing your full wealth potential?
2. As you analyze those self-limiting beliefs, where did they originate, and are they based on a lie, facts, or the truth?
3. What's the truth about your full wealth potential, and what new

experiences could you create to incorporate new beliefs about your full wealth potential?

4. When are you going to create those new experiences, so you can transcend the imaginary fences of what you've thought was possible for you, to experience an abundance of wealth in all 7 realms?
5. Is getting outside help to implement these strategies and create these new experiences something you're considering?

CONCLUSION

Starting Your **Wealth Building** Adventures

What To Do Next?

We've reached the end of our time together my friend. I've enjoyed every step of our journey together and I hope you've had more fun than I have.

To recap what we've covered:

1. In the first five chapters of this book, we explored why purpose is the key to being wealthy. We talked about how early retirement is a desirable objective for many, yet it shouldn't be your purpose. I believe you should Live Your Life on FIRE...Financially Independent and ReFired Early…even after you're technically Retired Early.

   You should live life 'RE-FIRED' about your purpose, and that's why we spent time making sure the readers of this book knew the importance of knowing your WHY, and we provided practical steps to help you discover both your Life and your Business Purpose

By now, you should have a clear picture on how to get fired up about your purpose, and why I say everything you desire in life can be found on the other side of truly discovering your purpose. It really is the key to being wealthy!

2. And, in the next five chapters of this book, we explored how to accelerate the creation of wealth. We started at the first logical place to do so, which is to find yourself a high income earning opportunity, and we made a case for why entrepreneurship was your best option for this.

   Then, we highlighted several things that could preclude you from accelerating the creation of wealth. In those discussions we defined what the "Mom and Dad Plan" is, and why it should be avoided.

   Next we pulled the veil on the perils of the financial services industry that you should be aware of. And, we talked about why you might want to "disown" your favorite Uncle…'Uncle Sam'...seeing he nevers sends you a Christmas present, but always delivers a dreaded tax bill right around Easter.

   Once you understood how to start on this journey with a high income earning opportunity in your quiver, we talked about the things you should avoid while on your way. Then, we concluded with the catalyst to get you to your intended destination in as little as 2 to 5 years by exposing you to my list of the top 9 wealth growth models for you to consider.

   At this point, you should be filled with a stream of consciousness of what it could look like to create massive amounts of wealth, even on a tax-free basis, should you desire to.

3. Then, in the final three chapters, we discussed how to guarantee your wealth success. That discussion started off with understanding the 5 reasons we fail to achieve our financial success.

   We even gave you a sneak peek at how we passively leverage 3 of the top 9 wealth growth models to shrink financial independence timelines from 30 years down to as little as 2 to 5 years for my clients.

Then, I showed you the 5 ways we guarantee our client's success while showing you the various guarantees reflected in the agreements of the clients who qualify to work with us.

I wrapped this section up by showing you what the Manifest Wealth Safely Method can do for you, by showing you how we help people who have $100,000 in liquid net worth, and those who have much less than that, get to a desired end, where they've added $1,000,000 in new wealth, and $100,000 in passive income, in 5 years or less.

I concluded this section with the 5 stages of our Program and also reminded you of the comments existing clients have shared that are a part of my Righteous Billionaire Movement and my Manifest Wealth Safely Program.

Each chapter in this book has included questions for reflection to help you internalize the concepts shared, as well as start thinking through how you will implement the information and strategies shared.

At this point, I'm going to share a principle I share with people whenever I speak or give a presentation. Here it is: "Information, without application, leads to devastation. But, Information, with application, always leads to transformation."

The next step for you is to simply create the transformation you desire from this information. To do so requires you do two things:

Take Action.

You take action by deciding if you want help in implementing the information you've just learned, or if you want to go it alone. But, the key is you must take action. Make one small decision right now on what action you'll take.

Take one action each and every day, and soon you'll see the ripple effect of those actions lead to transforming your financial picture in ways you could not imagine.

Five years from now, I'll be writing a book on how I became a Billionaire in 5 years. I assure you that one of the reasons why that will happen for me is because I took action.

As an author, I get emails and comments from people who tell me they love my books and are thankful that I wrote them.

Here's what I can say about that. If you would like to share your gratitude for me sharing this book with you, then do me a favor by simply taking action on the information I've shared with you.

Your transformation is the best kind of thank you that you can give to the creator of intellectual property, like that which is contained in this book.

If you decide you'd like our help in taking action on the information contained in this book, then schedule a time for us to have a chat at the link below:

http://call.manifestwealthsafely.com

We're good at what we do, just like you're good at what you do. Since we're good at what we do, we have a moral obligation to share our gift, and serve the world in every imaginable way possible.

That's what happens when you've discovered your WHY, and unlocked your purpose.

I wish the same for you!

To your abundant wealth,

Ike Ikokwu

"The Safe Wealth Creator"

Founder of the Righteous Billionaire Movement

Founder of the Manifest Wealth Safely Program

Founder of the Seven Figure Mentor Program

How To Get More Help

I've included a few extra resources for you to access as a reader of this book. It's part "thank you" and part "I didn't have enough room in the book, but I still want to teach it to you."

The links below will take you to privately hosted E-books and videos where you can access the additional training.

Also, I've included information and a link on how my team and I can help you with every step of The Manifest Wealth Safely Method. We have multiple offerings, from self assessments to discover your WHY Operating System, to group coaching sessions, to full-service done for you offerings, so you can passively add $1,000,000 in new wealth, and $100,000 in passive income, in 5 years or less. For more information please see the details below.

A Deep Dive Into The Mom and Dad Plan

You heard me introduce the Mom and Dad Plan to you and why you need to avoid it in chapter 7 of this book. What I shared was just a tip of the iceberg. For a deeper dive into the kind of financial havoc this plan is wrecking in the lives of massive amounts of individuals and families, you'll want to dig into the 38 page E-Book.

This E-Book was previously only available to clients of our financial coaching programs, but we've made it available to purchasers of this book.

Access this resource at the link below.

http://bookbonus.manifestwealthsafely.com

7 Steps To Experiencing Money & Life Abundantly

Did you know that money has a language all of its own? Everyday, money speaks to you, with just about every interaction you have with others and the world. If you are oblivious to what money is saying to you, or how you are knowingly and unknowingly reacting to the conversation it is having with you, your experience of money and life will be less than ideal.

This E-Book, and workbook, will help you completely transform your relationship with money, so you can experience it and life, in greater abundance.

Access this resource at the link below.

http://bookbonus.manifestwealthsafely.com

Solopreneur Seven Figure Blueprint

In chapter 5 of this book you were introduced to a 5 step process to discover your business purpose. And, in chapter 6, I shared how entrepreneurship can be your best option for finding a high-income earning opportunity.

In this video training, you'll discover how we help the clients in our Seven Figure Mentor Program, turn their annual income into a monthly income, enjoy 12 weeks off a year, and thrive without ever worrying about marketing again.

Access this resource at the link below.

http://bookbonus.manifestwealthsafely.com

Live Your Life On FIRE...Financially Independent & Retired Early

This entire book has been about how to help you use the manifest wealth safely method to create $1,000,000 in new wealth and $100,000 in passive income in 5 years or less, while pursuing purpose-driven passion projects you love, that can change the world.

In this video training, you'll get to reinforce what you've learned in this book, while doing a deep dive on: How To Live Your Life On FIRE...Financially Independent & Retired Early...So You Can Fulfill Your Purpose...While Enjoying Six Figures In Passive Income.

Access this resource at the link below

http://bookbonus.manifestwealthsafely.com

Work With Me And My Team To Accelerate Your Results

You've read testimonials from clients we're currently working with. We are always on the hunt for our next big client case study. If you love what you heard in this book, and want our help to add $1,000,000 in new wealth, and $100,000 in passive income, in 5 years or less, please book a call with me or a member of our team.

We offer a wide range of solutions, including DIY digital courses, group coaching programs, and completely done for you offers. Whatever your budget, we have a way of helping you implement The Manifest Wealth Safely Method, in your life today.

So, please don't wait. Book a call with us today at the link below. We want to help: **http://call.manifestwealthsafely.com**

About The Author

Having made and lost 7-Figures twice in his career, Ike brings very relevant experience to his role as a **Business Growth Strategist, Mindset Coach, and Personal Finance Expert** to his clients.

Working with two of the largest global coaching companies in the industry and leaning on wisdom gained from overcoming many adversities in life, Ike has the ability to change the way his clients think and feel about things, so they can create the results they truly desire.

Purpose-driven entrepreneurs, working professionals, and families hire him to shrink their financial independence timelines down from 30 years, to as little as 2 years, while growing as a leader.

Because most are frustrated with inept leadership within the fibers of our nation, they work hard, putting in long hours, all in the hopes of fulfilling their purpose and making a difference in our society, even though deep down they wonder if there's a better way.

Due to the curve balls of life, many of Ike's clients feel like they are behind the "8-Ball," when it comes to securing their financial future. So, through his proprietary process, Ike shows them how to earn 1% to 25% monthly returns on their wealth, to make up for all of that "lost" time.

Ike helps them leverage the secrets of top tier financial institutions, and family offices, to manifest wealth safely and quickly, so they can accelerate the positive changes they want to make in their communities.

Bottom line is: Ike empowers visionary entrepreneurs, working professionals, and families with the leadership and financial capital to make purpose-driven and legacy-impacting changes to their nations and communities as world changers.

Ike is a Best-Selling Author, the Founder and Entrepreneurial Dream Reviver at The Coachanaire Institute (TCI), Founder of the Righteous Billionaire Movement (RBM), Founder of the Manifest Wealth Safely Program (MWSP), and the Seven Figure Mentor Program (7FMP)

All inquiries for podcast appearances, video shows, and speaking can be sent to **help@winningthemoneygame.net**